SIR WILLIAM OSLER

Medical Humanist

William Osler as a young professor of medicine at McGill University, Montreal.
SOURCE: The Osler Library, McGill University

❦ SIR WILLIAM OSLER ❧

Medical Humanist

PHILIP W. LEON

HERITAGE BOOKS
2007

HERITAGE BOOKS
AN IMPRINT OF HERITAGE BOOKS, INC.

Books, CDs, and more—Worldwide

For our listing of thousands of titles see our website
at
www.HeritageBooks.com

Published 2007 by
HERITAGE BOOKS, INC.
Publishing Division
65 East Main Street
Westminster, Maryland 21157-5026

Copyright © 2007 Philip W. Leon, Ph.D.

Other books by the author:
Nanny Wood: From Washington Belle to Portland's Grande Dame

Text designed by Dianna Rich and set in Classic Garamond
Cover designed by Kevin Metzger
Author Photo by Russ Pace
Cover: Sir William Osler, 1913.
Courtesy of McMaster University Health Sciences Foundation
This book was made possible by a grant from
The Citadel Foundation.

All rights reserved. No part of this book may be reproduced or transmitted in any form or by any means, electronic or mechanical, including photocopying, recording or by any information storage and retrieval system without written permission from the author, except for the inclusion of brief quotations in a review.

International Standard Book Number: 978-0-7884-3397-0

This book is dedicated to

THE AMERICAN OSLER SOCIETY

THE OSLER CLUB OF LONDON

THE JAPANESE OSLER SOCIETY

CONTENTS

Preface		ix
Acknowledgments		xv
Chapter I	WALT WHITMAN	1
Chapter II	THOMAS EAKINS	17
Chapter III	MARK TWAIN	29
Chapter IV	THOMAS LOVELL BEDDOES	43
Chapter V	SARAH ORNE JEWETT	59
Chapter VI	HENRY JAMES & EDITH WHARTON	73
Chapter VII	ROBERT BROWNING	93
Chapter VIII	NATHAN SMITH	111
Chapter IX	WHITELAW REID	121
Chapter X	JOHN KEATS	131
Chapter XI	JOHN DONNE	147
Works Cited		161
Index		167

PREFACE

In the *Los Angeles Times* of 16 August 1896, a half-page display advertisement appeared for a local group of five medical doctors, called the "English and German Expert Specialists." The ad's bold headline declares, "Magnificent Indorsement," and goes on to claim, "America's grandest physician, PROF. WILLIAM OSLER, M.D., F.R.C.P.S., Eng., author of the greatest medical text book in the world, and professor in the Johns Hopkins University, America's foremost educational institution, indorses the English and German Expert Specialists." Osler almost certainly did not provide this "indorsement"—it would have been most uncharacteristic—although he might have sent a note wishing success to his former student at McGill University, Dr. T.J.P. O'Brien, one of the five redundantly titled "expert specialists." The group claimed to cure chronic catarrh for "$5.00 per Month—Medicines Free."

Below this large ad appears a smaller one for a $1.25 bottle of "McBurney's Kidney & Bladder Cure," one bottle of which was guaranteed to cure any disease of the bladder, bed-wetting in children, gall stones, diabetes, and "thick, turbid urine." Positioned beside McBurney's ad is one for "Ghirardelli's Cocoa," which "makes puny children stout and hearty," an ideal drink for "all who want health, strength, steady nerves and a cheerful disposition."

The grandiose claims of the "expert specialists" not only acknowledge William Osler's prominence as "America's grandest physician," but also serve, along with the smaller ads, as an extended metaphor for the state of medicine in the United States and Canada at the turn of the century. Patent medicines, nostrums, snake-oil treatments—call them what you will—had been a mainstay of medical treatments in the nineteenth century, owing largely to their opium and alcohol bases that provided temporary relief from pain but effected no cure. As the end of the century approached, a better educated public was coming to understand that these touted panaceas were worthless while the medical profession, represented here by Osler, was advancing rapidly from guesswork to scientifically based treatment.

Osler had for over twenty years been gaining an international reputation in a profession that often fastened its faith in a medical treatment onto the individual who discovered a disease or who developed a specific treatment or who, as did Osler, inspired confidence in his colleagues through insightful publication and teaching. The pantheon existing in Osler's time included the ancient Galen and later Vesalius on anatomy; William Harvey on the circulation of blood; Thomas Sydenham on clinical diagnosis; Edward Jenner on vaccination; Joseph Lister on antisepsis and asepsis; Louis Pasteur on infectious diseases; Rudolf Virchow on cellular pathology; and Robert Koch on bacteriology. Pulling together these and other medical pioneers from disparate times and places, Osler's textbook and other writings qualified him for inclusion on the list of immortal physicians.

In 1892, with his publication of *The Principles and Practice of Medicine*, Osler became the premier medical authority at a time when hard-working, sincere researchers and practitioners were in pursuit of the nature of infection, disease etiology, and specific cures for both acute and chronic illness. For the next forty years his textbook was the standard for all medical instruction in North America, England, Europe, and Asia, translated into Russian, French, German,

Chinese, Spanish, and Portugese. The various editions comprised a publication record of a half-million copies. When he died in 1919, he was the best-known and most widely respected medical doctor in the world.

Oslerians, devotees worldwide of this exemplary man, know his history. Born in Bond Head, Ontario, Canada, in 1849, the son of an Anglican clergyman, Osler received his education first at the University of Toronto where he thought he might pursue the ministry, and at McGill University in Montreal where he fulfilled his passion for medicine, taking his M.D. in 1872. He was recruited away from his post as a professor in the medical school at McGill to the University of Pennsylvania in 1884. In Philadelphia he continued to build his international reputation by reading papers at conferences in England and on the Continent. In 1889 he left Philadelphia to assume the position of physician-in-chief at the newly founded Johns Hopkins medical school; he completed the writing of *The Principles and Practice of Medicine* while the university hired staff and faculty and acquired equipment. In 1905 Osler assumed the chair of Regius Professor of Medicine at Oxford University, a position that allowed him to travel, publish, and further influence the profession of medicine. In 1911 King George V created him a baronet, and he became "Sir William Osler, Bart."

This sketch of his life hardly captures the spirit of Osler and his ability to inspire both students and colleagues, but outstanding biographies are available to attest to his remarkable life. Today, writings about Osler form a hagiography; his status in the medical profession approaches sainthood; the invocation of his name elicits an adoration that is sincere and heartfelt by people who never knew him. Words that Oslerians frequently use to describe him include charismatic, optimistic, generous, caring, and industrious. The Osler Club of London (founded 1928), the American

Osler Society (founded 1970), and the Japanese Osler Club (founded 1983) are the principal organizations that perpetuate his memory and his ideals. He has come to symbolize all that is good and praiseworthy in a physician. McGill University's Osler Library, which houses his ashes immured behind a bronze plaque, has become a shrine to which every Oslerian, including myself, unashamedly enjoys making a pilgrimage.

Harvey Cushing's Pulitzer Prize-winning biography *The Life of Sir William Osler* (1925) began the seemingly endless succession of books published in Osler's honor. In 1976 appeared *An Annotated Checklist of Osleriana* by Earl F. Nation, Charles G. Roland, and John P. McGovern, all founding members of the American Osler Society. Charles S. Bryan's *Osler: Inspirations from a Great Physician* (1997) brings together contemporary social and personal issues with examples from Osler's writings indicating possible solutions to today's problems. In 1999, Michael Bliss, a distinguished historian at the University of Toronto, published *William Osler: A Life in Medicine,* a valuable biography revealing through anecdotes a more accessible and personal Osler than Cushing's earlier biography. Also in 1999, Richard Golden, a prolific Osler scholar, published *The Works of Egerton Yorrick Davis, MD; Sir William Osler's Alter Ego,* a delightful editing of Osler's humorous, often ribald writings under the pseudonym E.Y. Davis. In 2003, Mark E. Silverman, T. Jock Murray, and Charles S. Bryan edited *The Quotable Osler*, assembling his quotations, epigrams and other memorable sayings. In 2004, Richard Golden published *A History of William Osler's "The Principles and Practice of Medicine,"* lovingly describing every known version of the many editions. Clearly interest in Osler remains high.

Osler's motto on his coat of arms, "Aequanimitas," has become a mantra for Oslerians seeking to emulate his successful blending of personal and public life. This book offers a glimpse at the humanistic side of Osler, the side that balanced his medical endeavors. In calling Osler a medical humanist, I turn to F.C.S. Schiller's *Humanism* (1903); Osler's Oxford colleague, Schiller defined a humanist as one "keenly interested in the rich variety of human thought and sentiment" (xxi). Osler's interests extended far beyond medicine into many areas, but none more dear to him than literature, from the ancients to the contemporary. Osler was the only physician elected president of the British Classical Association. The subjects of his wide reading included authors who were both physicians and writers, among them François Rabelais, a French humanist; Thomas Lovell Beddoes, English poet and playwright; Sir Thomas Browne, English author of *Religio Medici*; John Keats, English Romantic poet and apothecary-surgeon; and John Brown, a Scottish essayist.

Osler knew many famous writers of his day. He treated Walt Whitman for five years. He knew Mark Twain, socializing with him in Canada and England. He knew the American short story writer Sarah Orne Jewett. Edith Wharton arranged for Osler to treat Henry James in London. Rudyard Kipling became a good friend. He knew America's greatest Realist painter, Thomas Eakins. He frequently enjoyed the company of ambassadors and statesmen who had occasion to visit Oxford.

This book is not an Osler biography. Rather, it is a collection of essays originally presented to gatherings of Oslerians at the Royal College of Physicians (London), the Royal College of Physicians (Edinburgh), Montreal, Toronto, San Francisco, Kansas City, and elsewhere, that seeks to illuminate Osler's special interest in the humanities. I intend this book for medical humanists, medical historians, and all those interested in the relationship of literature and medicine.

ACKNOWLEDGMENTS

I wish to acknowledge the contributions of several people and organizations that assisted with this book. Pamela J. Miller, History of Medicine Librarian, at the Osler Library of the History of Medicine, McGill University, granted permission to publish letters to Osler from G. Lytton Strachey, Dr. K. Hoffman, Edmund Gosse, and T. P. Beddoes. She also granted permission to use letters from T. P. Beddoes to Dr. Frey and Revell Phillips, as well as permission to quote from newspaper clippings inserted into Osler's copy of John Donne's *Biathanatos*.

Dr. Carl Spadoni, William Ready Division of Archives and Research Collections at McMaster University, Hamilton, Ontario, kindly provided the cover photo of Osler.

At The Citadel, Charleston, South Carolina, I want to thank Dr. Donald Steven, Provost of the college, for his support. In the English department, Dr. Jim Leonard and Libby Walker were particularly helpful. I also want to thank the staff at the Daniel Library, The Citadel, for their assistance in obtaining material. The Citadel Foundation, as always, was most generous in funding my research trips and enabled me to present papers on Osler at the Royal College of Physicians (London), the Royal College of Physicians (Edinburgh), in Toronto, Montreal, San Francisco, Kansas City, Washington, DC, and Los Angeles.

CHAPTER ONE

Osler and Walt Whitman

FROM 1885 TO 1889 WILLIAM OSLER provided medical care to the celebrated American poet Walt Whitman. Osler had recently been recruited as a professor at the University of Pennsylvania medical school in Philadelphia, just across the Delaware River from Camden, New Jersey, where Whitman had lived since 1884. The two became acquainted when Dr. Richard Maurice Bucke (1837–1902), director of the London (Ontario) Asylum for the Insane, asked his friend Osler to go over to Camden to check on the aged poet.

RICHARD MAURICE BUCKE

Before Dr. Bucke became an apostle of Whitman, he achieved prominence as a doctor at the McGill University medical school in Montreal; he finished at the top of his class in 1862, winning the prize for the best thesis, years before Osler would become a student and professor there. After taking his medical degree, he established himself within the profession as an innovative psychiatrist or "alienist"— mentally disturbed patients were considered alienated from normal behavior. His colleagues recognized his achievements when they elected Bucke to the Royal Society of Canada and later as the president of the American Psychiatric Association.

Osler and his colleagues at McGill University always

enjoyed hearing Bucke talk about Whitman on his visits to the medical school there. They regarded Bucke not only as a superb medical practitioner but also as a mystic, an odd but harmless character, whose regard for Whitman approached the kind of adoration usually reserved for a god or messiah. Bucke's most recent biographer says Bucke "saw in Whitman the incarnation of modern man, the prophet with a new and purer vision of the world."[1]

Bucke edited or wrote a dozen books about Whitman, emphasizing the poet's mystical qualities. As Bucke and Whitman grew closer over the years, Bucke adopted a Whitman-like persona, becoming almost his double in appearance. He adopted the wide-brimmed, floppy hat, the full, gray beard, and open-necked, comfortable clothing that we so often see in photographs of Whitman.

As the superintendent of the London Asylum for the Insane, Bucke instituted innovative and compassionate treatment for the patients. When he observed that the daily ministrations of the male attendants frequently caused the patients to behave violently, he introduced female attendants into the male ward, despite warnings that the patients would sexually assault the women or at the least expose themselves and commit other unspeakable outrages. The male patients became surprisingly shy and calm in the presence of the women attendants. Embarrassed to be considered crude, the patients began to clean their rooms and to attend to personal grooming without the contentiousness that characterized their reactions to orders from the male staff.

Bucke wanted to improve the patients' feelings of self-worth, so he arranged jobs for them at the asylum and in the nearby community; some were given wages. He also engaged carpenters to install superfluous doors leading from the wards to the grounds. This abundance of unnecessary doors gave the patients a sense of freedom and openness, fostering the idea that they were, indeed, patients, not prisoners.

Most dramatic of all, Bucke eliminated alcohol as a sedative. The standard practice in most insane asylums in North America at that time was to administer intoxicating doses of cheap alcohol each morning, thereby keeping the patients in a stupor for most of the day. This daily dosing amounted to an admission by the doctors that a cure was impossible and that the most efficacious treatment would be to keep the patients calm and sedated—less trouble for everyone.

At separate times both Whitman and Osler visited the London Asylum for the Insane and praised Bucke's initiatives. Whitman went there as a personal guest of Bucke, and Osler visited as part of a medical inspection team that came away with high praise for Bucke and his advances in the treatment of the mentally ill.

COSMIC CONSCIOUSNESS

Bucke's great work, *Cosmic Consciousness,* published in 1901 and never once out of print, discusses various "geniuses" from history who achieved greatness through their mystical liberation. According to Bucke, Whitman and others had, as representatives of a vanguard of human evolution, experienced an "illumination" and developed a "consciousness of the cosmos" which augured well for the future of humanity. The individuals whom Bucke describes in *Cosmic Consciousness* have arrived at a higher spiritual plane than ordinary mortals. Included in his book are chapters on Gautama the Buddha, Jesus the Christ, Paul, Plotinus, Mohammed, Dante, William Blake, and, of course, Walt Whitman. The practical-minded Osler had difficulty embracing Bucke's esoteric theories, but he bought two copies of Bucke's book through friendship.

Bucke's own "illumination" into cosmic consciousness occurred after reading Whitman's poetry. Writing in the third person, he gave this account of how he arrived at the rapturous moment:

> It was in the early spring at the beginning of his thirty-sixth year. He and two friends had spent the evening reading Wordsworth, Shelley, Keats, Browning, and especially Whitman. They parted at midnight, and he had a long drive in a hansom (it was in an English city). His mind, deeply under the influence of the ideas, images and emotions called up by the reading and talk of the evening, was calm and peaceful. He was in a state of quiet, almost passive enjoyment. All at once, without warning of any kind, he found himself wrapped around as it were by a flame colored cloud. For an instant he thought of fire, some sudden conflagration in the great city, the next he knew that the light was within himself. Directly afterwards came upon him a sense of exultation, of immense joyousness accompanied or immediately followed by an intellectual illumination quite impossible to describe. Into his brain streamed one momentary lightning-flash of the Brahmic Splendor which has ever since lightened his life; upon his heart fell one drop of Brahmic Bliss, leaving thenceforward for always an after taste of heaven.[2]

Although Osler never shared Bucke's apotheosis of Whitman, he generously provided medical attention to Whitman as a favor to his friend Bucke, visiting Whitman almost monthly without any fee for five years. Sometimes he would take a younger colleague or student with him on his visits. Often he would take a book or some other small present that he thought Whitman might enjoy. Osler and Silas Weir Mitchell, the brilliant neurologist arranged for Nathan M. Baker, a medical student at Pennsylvania, to serve as a nurse who visited Whitman almost daily until he received his M.D. degree and moved away.

Osler arrived in Philadelphia in October 1884, and shortly after his arrival he visited Whitman but treatment was not necessary on this first visit. He thought Whitman looked majestic and instantly liked him. Whitman's first recorded mention of his receiving medical attention from Osler occurs in his *Commonplace Book*, where he wrote that on 19 October 1885 Osler accompanied him to see the noted ophthalmologist Dr. William F. Norris: "Satisfactory visit and examination—I had feared I was becoming blind. Dr. N. decidedly discountenanced the idea."[3] Referrals were becoming a standard part of medical practice as specialties developed at the turn of the century.[4] That Osler knew his limitations for treating eye problems and personally escorted Whitman to Dr. Norris indicates that Whitman was receiving the best treatment available because of Osler's selflessness.

One of the most dramatic incidents of Osler's attendance on Whitman occurred on Sunday morning, 10 June 1888. In Philadelphia visiting the Norristown Asylum, Bucke had dined with Osler at the Rittenhouse Club the night before. When Bucke called on Whitman on Sunday, he found his friend showing signs of great distress. Whitman's housekeeper Mary O. Davis and his daily visitor Horace Traubel became alarmed. At Bucke's direction, Traubel raced over to Philadelphia but could not find Osler, neither in his rooms, nor his office, nor at the Rittenhouse, nor at the University Club. Traubel was not aware that Osler customarily toured the wards on Sunday morning when the hospital would be quiet and less frantic than on a weekday. Bucke finally found Osler later in the day and accompanied him over the river to Camden. Although a medical doctor himself, Bucke never treated Whitman as Osler had done, and his specialty in psychiatry rendered him unsuitable to attend to a patient who might be suffering from a stroke or some other serious physical ailment. Finding the old poet in bed, confused and slurring his speech, Osler thought the symptoms indicated sclerosis of the arteries of the brain. Nothing medically could be done except to observe the patient and make him comfortable. Whitman improved gradually, and in about a week he had fully recovered.

Although grateful for Osler's care, Whitman did not always like his inevitably cheerful view. Osler lore holds that he became the model of the caring doctor whose bedside manner exuded warmth and conveyed confidence to the patient that all would be well. Horace Traubel records Whitman's thoughts in September 1888: "Osler made light of my condition. I don't like his pooh-poohs: the professional air of the doctor grates on me."[5] When Bucke attempted to mollify Whitman by telling him that Osler's medical opinion merited the highest credibility and should be trusted, Whitman responded, "I confess I do not wholly like or credit what he says—I do not fancy the jaunty way in which he seems inclined to dismiss the troubles."[6]

Osler's career was on the ascendancy, and his professional and personal relationship with Whitman ended when he accepted a position in May 1889 as Physician-in-Chief at the new medical school at the John Hopkins University in Baltimore where he wrote his pathbreaking textbook, *The Principles and Practice of Medicine* (1892) which became the standard medical text for at least four decades.[7]

Osler's time in Philadelphia was notable for his growing reputation as a master teacher and researcher, a clinician of the first order. Years later, as he stood at the pinnacle of his career as Regius Professor of Medicine at Oxford, Osler looked back with affection at the time he spent with America's greatest poet, Walt Whitman.

OSLER AND WHITMAN IN ENGLAND

In 1918, having been at Oxford since 1905, Osler was at work on a "Personal Reminiscence" of the five years that he spent treating and getting to know Walt Whitman, a lecture to be delivered at Oxford and at the City Temple. When Osler began preparing his "Personal Reminiscences" of Walt Whitman, he remembered that in 1891 Bucke had served as a personal emissary from Whitman to the Bolton College, which was not a college at all in the present sense of the term. The Bolton College consisted of a group of socialists living near Manchester who found in Whitman's *Leaves of Grass* the clearest expression of their democratic ideals. Numbering over the years on average fifteen to twenty-five members and composed of weavers, clerks, ministers, millwrights, and others, the Boys of the Bolton College, as they called themselves, felt that Whitman spoke directly to them in the voice of the working class.

The principal leaders of the College were J. W. Wallace, an architect's assistant; Dr. John Johnston, a general practitioner; Charles F. Sixsmith, the manager of Bentinck Mill in Farnworth; Fred Wild, a cotton-waste dealer; Richard Greenhalgh, a bank clerk; William Law, an accountant; Sam Hodgkinson, a hosiery manufacturer; William Pimblett, an engineering firm's federation secretary; Reverend Tyas; Reverend F. R. C. Hutton, vicar of the St. George's Congregational Church; Thomas Shorrock, a magistrate's clerk; Wentworth Dixon, a lawyer's clerk; Reverend Scott of Harwood Unitarian church; George Humphreys, a working millwright; and W. M. Carr, an architect.[8]

Three causes united the Bolton College: their adoration

for Whitman and the ideas expressed in *Leaves of Grass,* their passionate belief in socialism's superiority to capitalism, and their varyingly explicit homosexuality. We can understand these three aspects of the group when we take a look at its three principal leaders: Dr. John Johnston, J. W. Wallace, and C. F. Sixsmith.

DR. JOHN JOHNSTON

I have discovered direct communication between Osler and Johnston and Wallace, both of whom had visited Whitman in Camden and wrote a subsequent book, *Visits to Walt Whitman in Camden in 1890–91.* Osler donated his personal copy of this book to the Tudor and Stuart Club collection at the Johns Hopkins University in memory of his son Revere. In that copy I found several items reflecting Osler's direct correspondence in 1889 and 1919 with the leaders of the Bolton College.

Apparently Dr. Johnston, a general practitioner, could be a self-promoter, and he enjoyed his status as one of the better educated men in the College. He was not shy about sending Osler a clipping from the *Annandale Observer,* 26 October 1917, providing his biography, including his service during World War I. The article closes by saying that "the Doctor has traveled much, and has delighted many Bolton and Annan audiences with his lectures and scenes at home and abroad. He has published many pamphlets descriptive of his foreign travels . . . while his book 'A Visit to Walt Whitman' [sic] is well known to all lovers of 'The Good Grey Poet.'"

In the inside back cover of this book I found placed there by Osler a reprint from the London *Times Literary Supplement,* 3 January 1918, of an unsigned review of Johnston and Wallace's book. The reviewer declared the

Bolton College group as the equal of "great fires of intellectual life which burn at Oxford and at Cambridge." The lengthy review is wholly favorable, both in its respectful tone toward Whitman and in its assessment of the contents and quality of writing on the part of both authors.

Johnston sent Osler two other items which Osler placed in his book. The first is an article by Johnston from the *Grange Guardian,* entitled "On Yewbarrow Crag on Christmas Day, 1917." Johnston says that as he sits looking out over Yewbarrow Crag he is "strongly conscious of the personal presence of . . . my great camerado Walt Whitman, cheering and blessing upon this Christmas morn." The article quotes a passage of Whitman's poetry which lends itself to the socialist cause, and Johnston concludes by saying, "Let us hope that Whitman's lines are prophetic and that the capitalistic age is passing away." Johnston blended Christ, Whitman, and socialism in a most unique manner. The second item preserved by Osler is a letter, dated 18 January 1918, from Johnston to Osler:

Sir William Osler, Bt., LL.D., Etc.,
13 Norham Gardens, Oxford.

My Dear Sir,
It is very good of you to send such a nice Letter about our Book, "Visits to Walt Whitman," and I thank you cordially for your expression of appreciation and for your kind greetings to Mr. Wallace and myself.

I am sorry I have not a spare copy of my own "Notes of a Visit to Walt Whitman and some of his friends, in 1890"—the book has long been out of print.

It is interesting to have your reminder of your attendance upon Walt in the 1888–89 illness (which, of course, I knew of), and of your friendship with Dr. Bucke.

It may interest you to know that our Book is now in its Second Edition—although it was only published December 11th 1917, and it was hailed as a "venture of faith" and prophesied to prove a failure—owing to the War Conditions being so infavourable to such a book.

I am glad to know that you have such a good collection of "Whitmaniana," and it may interest you to know that Mr. Wallace and I—with the help of Mr. Saunders of Toronto—are trying to induce all the possessors of such material to bequeath it to some Central Public Institution for permanent preservation, instead of its being allowed to be scattered all over the world—to form a Permanent Museum of Whitman materiel. In this Scheme we have the active cooperation and assistance of Edward Carpenter and many other Whitmanites, who have promised to so dispose of their collections—and I should be glad if we could be favoured with your active sympathy and support.

Please accept of my best thanks for your kind invitation to your Home at Oxford, which I should be glad of the opportunity of one day being able to accept.

Again thanking you for your good words *re* our book, and with kinds regards and all good wishes,

I remain,
Yours sincerely,
J Johnston[9]

This letter reveals that Osler was cordial and generous to his fellow medical doctor, but no record exists indicating that Johnston ever visited Osler at Oxford or Osler venturing north to Bolton. Osler appears to have initiated contact with the leaders of the Bolton group. Johnston would certainly have known of Osler's extensive association with Whitman back in Camden, and since Johnston and Osler were both medical doctors, one might assume that Johnston would have been eager to meet Osler at Oxford or to invite him to come up to Bolton for a meeting of the College, but their relationship never progressed beyond this correspondence, perhaps owing to Osler's failing health.

J. W. WALLACE

The second guiding figure in the group and one of the most radically socialistic was J. W. Wallace, called "the Master of the College." Born in 1853, Wallace was the son of an English millwright who had worked in Russia. Lacking formal education, when he was fourteen years old, Wallace went to work as an architect's assistant and remained with that same firm until his retirement in 1912. Dr. Bucke, in his *Cosmic Consciousness,* devotes a chapter to Wallace and says that he, too, had this special cosmic insight.

Wallace supplied a testimonial to Dr. Bucke for inclusion in *Cosmic Consciousness.* In it, Wallace says that when his mother died in 1885 ("the heaviest grief and pain I have ever known, or shall, probably ever know"), he found solace in *Leaves of Grass,* finding "the deep thrill of contact with a mighty spirit. And it seemed a great thing that [Whitman], of all men, taught the doctrine of immortality with quite new emphasis and authority."

Still living at home with his mother and father at age 31, Wallace apparently struggled with his sexual identity. He confessed that he had "many grave faults and strong opposing idiosyncrasies" that "my own tastes and pursuits kept me more closely at home than is the case with most young men." His father was frequently away from home for long periods, and Wallace became the object of his mother's affection. He became her "ruling passion—a deep, constant, absorbing and self-sacrificing love."[10]

Largely through the influence of Wallace, Whitman

became an icon for democracy and brotherhood for English readers. Although Wallace supported the Russian Revolution of 1917, he deplored violence and felt that Whitman's doctrine of love and comradeship would guide British socialism in the right direction.

Wallace appears to have had some confused sexual longings. On most of the Bolton College Whitman Birthday celebrations each May, Wallace would read aloud some of Whitman's poems containing his most explicit phallic and homoerotic imagery. And yet, for a time at least, Wallace fell in love with Katherine Conway, a popular and attractive socialist who became close to the Bolton group. Conway did not return Wallace's affection, marrying instead Bruce Glasier, a leader in the Independent Labour Party and a close associate of Keir Hardie, the "Father of British Socialism." Wallace was disappointed by Katherine's marriage, but became friends with Bruce Glasier and remained on good terms with them both. The Glasiers provided Wallace with an organized movement and encouraged him to spread the doctrine of socialism by speaking of Whitman at their rallies.

Osler and Wallace also had direct communication. A letter of 4 May 1919 from Wallace asks Osler to send a letter in praise of Whitman to organizers of a centennial celebration of Whitman in America. When Wallace wrote this letter Osler was working assiduously, despite bad health, to complete his presidential address for the British Classical Association, "The Old Humanities and the New Science." This important lecture consumed his time, thus he was unable to send the requested tribute. He had temporarily put aside his unfinished "Reminiscences" of Whitman; however, he resumed the task and wrote this letter to Wallace in September:

Sep. 23, 1919

J. W. Wallace, Esq., Chorley.

I was preparing a centenary lecture on Walt Whitman with my personal reminiscences to be given here in the school of English literature, but I have now to postpone it until next year. I wrote asking Johnston whether he thought W. W. had ever got into touch with the leaders and thinkers of English democracy. You will have heard of course of the death of Horace Traubel [Whitman's amanuensis who recorded his daily activities and published them as *With Walt Whitman in Camden*] . . . it was not always easy to see how much was Whitman and how much was Traubel. As Weir Mitchell [the Philadelphia neurologist] remarked about his first book, it is less a "biography than the autobiography of the biographer."

Sincerely yours,
Wm. Osler

Wallace replied on 6 October 1919 to Osler's letter with commentary on the deplorable lack of devotion to Whitman by the current leaders of British socialism: "I found them fairly responsive to the social implications of his message and his personality, but with only a limited grasp of his real significance, and of the orbic range of his vision." In response to Osler's remarks about Horace Traubel and *With Walt Whitman in Camden*, which mentions Osler frequently in accounts of his visits to check on the state of Whitman's health, Wallace says, "I have read every word of Walt's references to you, and have noted with great pleasure his high regard for you, both as a doctor and as a man. All I know of you justifies it, and I am sure that if I met you my own affection would go out to 'the human critter' which with Walt always ranked first."[11]

CHARLES F. SIXSMITH

In addition to the fervent socialism and reverence for the poetry of Whitman, there can be little doubt that homosexuality, whether practiced or simply discussed, was the third essential theme for the Bolton College. The third leader of the Bolton College group was Charles F. Sixsmith, a bisexual. Sixsmith, who was married and had children, "outraged his neighbours by love-making in the garden!"[12] In 1891, Bucke traveled to England to meet Tennyson and to see his fellow Whitmanites in Bolton. When Bucke visited the group he brought with him the openly homosexual clergyman, writer, and literary critic Edward Carpenter. Carpenter claimed to have had a sexual relationship with Walt Whitman on a visit to Camden, but this claim is unlikely because of the constant presence of Whitman's coterie. In a letter to Carpenter, Sixsmith says, "Women attract me, and yet full intercourse has not satisfied me, and I prefer the company of men, and can be attracted to them also. But really I am the greatest puzzle to myself, a bundle of paradoxes and contradictions."[13] Dr. John Johnston wrote in his diary that he and Carpenter frequently discussed "sexual inversion," as homosexuality was then called. Sixsmith and Carpenter, and perhaps Wallace and Johnston, found the Bolton College a suitable forum for their sexual proclivities as well as their political and social views.

CONCLUSION

Osler was intrigued and amused by the way his old friend and patient Whitman had been appropriated by special interest groups both in America and in England. Bucke and the members of the Bolton College appear to have grafted onto *Leaves of Grass* their particular spiritual, political, and sexual persuasions. Osler kept a respectful distance from Bucke's view of *Leaves of Grass* as a thematic and symbolic complement to his personal, cosmic mysticism. Nor did Osler embrace the Bolton College's radical socialism, their belief in Whitman as messiah, and the homosexuality present in varying measures by the members of the group. Osler's involvement with the group grew out of his honest friendship with Bucke and Whitman, two older men whom he genuinely liked for their personal warmth.

Osler corresponded with Johnston and Wallace in order to obtain fresh insight into Walt Whitman as he prepared his lecture with his characteristic thoroughness. Osler's health deteriorated shortly after his correspondence with Johnston and Wallace in 1919, and his "Personal Reminiscences of Walt Whitman" were, alas, never completed and the lecture never delivered.

NOTES

[1] Peter Rechnitzer, *R. M. Bucke: Journey to Cosmic Consciousness* (Markham, Ontario: Fitzhenry & Whiteside, 1994), 233.

[2] Richard Maurice Bucke, *Cosmic Consciousness* (New York: Citadel Press, 1993), 7–8.

[3] Walt Whitman, *The Correspondence: Walt Whitman*, ed. Edwin Haviland Miller (New York: NYU Press, 1964), 3: 406n.

[4] Christopher Crenner, *Private Practice: In the Early Twentieth-Century Medical Office of Dr. Richard Cabot* (Baltimore: The Johns Hopkins University Press, 2005), 58.

[5] Horace Traubel, *With Walt Whitman in Camden* (New York: Rowman and Littlefield, 1961), 2: 383.

[6] Traubel, 2: 432.

[7] Richard L. Golden, *A History of William Osler's "The Principles and Practice of Medicine"* (Montreal: Osler Library, 200), xii.

[8] Philip W. Leon, *Walt Whitman and Sir William Osler* (Toronto: ECW Press, 1995), 119.

[9] This letter is housed in the Milton S. Eisenhower Library at the Johns Hopkins University, Baltimore.

[10] Bucke, 279.

[11] This letter is housed in the Osler Library at McGill University, Montreal.

[12] Paul Salveson, *Loving Comrades: Lancashire's Links to Walt Whitman* (Bolton, Eng.: Worker's Educational Association, 1984), 13.

[13] Salveson, 13.

CHAPTER TWO

Osler and Thomas Eakins

SIR WILLIAM OSLER KNEW the American Realist artist Thomas Eakins (1844–1916), who painted dozens of distinguished members of the Philadelphia medical community. Art critics today place Eakins in the top tier of American artists; many ascribe to him the title of "America's greatest Realist" (while others argue in favor of Mary Cassatt). Osler's ties with Eakins are extensive, and an examination of their relationship reveals that Eakins, like Walt Whitman and Mark Twain, was not only exceedingly interesting but also that he could be controversial.

Osler and Eakins saw each other frequently at Whitman's home in Camden, New Jersey, when Eakins painted the poet's portrait in 1887 and 1888, the time when Osler regularly visited Whitman to care for his medical needs. Although Osler had nothing to do with the painting of Whitman's portrait, he does have strong connections with two of Eakins's most famous pictures, *The Gross Clinic* and *The Agnew Clinic,* and he was well acquainted with dozens of medical men who sat for portraits by Eakins.

EAKINS'S EARLY CAREER

Eakins lived in Philadelphia all his life with the exception of about five years when he studied art in Europe. At the Central High School he received his first instruction in anatomy, a necessary course for art students.[1] Eakins became so fascinated with the study of anatomy that he seriously considered changing his life's work and becoming a surgeon. In 1862, he enrolled in anatomy classes offered by the Pennsylvania Academy of Fine Arts, an institution with which he was later to have stormy relations, then two years later he registered for a more demanding course at Thomas Jefferson Medical College where he was called upon to practice dissection alongside the medical students. This intensive investigation into the musculature and skeletal constructions provided him with an education essential for a portraitist.

The course at Jefferson made Eakins realize that he needed more instruction if he intended to wed art and anatomy, and, in 1866, he left for Paris. To improve his understanding of anatomy, he observed surgical clinics at Paris hospitals and at the École de Médicine.[2] At this point in his career he had already achieved a degree of sophistication in the study of anatomy that many physicians in North America would envy.

For his art training, he studied at the École des Beaux-Arts with Jean-Léon Gérôme, with portraitist Léon Bonnat, and with sculptor Augustin-Alexandre Dumont.[3] After three productive years in Paris, Eakins went to Spain for further study where he assimilated the styles of Velásquez (1599–1660) and Ribera (1591–1652); he returned to Philadelphia in 1870.

Five years after he returned from Europe, Eakins undertook one of his greatest paintings, one that was to shake the comfortable world of American art in the way that Whitman's *Leaves of Grass,* two decades earlier, had jolted the world of American poetry.

THE GROSS CLINIC

The Gross Clinic (1875), the violently realistic depiction of Dr. Samuel D. Gross in an operating theatre, involved Eakins in one of the greatest imbroglios of the American art world in the nineteenth century. Samuel David Gross (1805–84) graduated from Thomas Jefferson Medical College, and, having built a brilliant career in various cities, returned to the college in 1856 to become the Chair of Institutes and Practice of Surgery, a post he held until 1882. During the Civil War, Gross wrote an influential manual of military surgery. Not only was Gross admired in the Philadelphia medical community, but also he was widely known throughout America and in Europe. By the time Eakins painted his portrait, Gross's abilities had earned him the sobriquet of "The Emperor of American Surgery."[4] He was a monumental figure whose widely anticipated portrait was expected to be dignified, staid, and proper, but the final product was so unorthodox that it was barred from being shown in the art galleries of the Centennial Exposition of 1876 and relegated, instead, to an exhibit of a model ward of a U.S. Army hospital. This snub by the selection jury triggered the first skirmish in a war with the artistic authorities that continued throughout Eakins's career.

Critics reacted with hostility to the painting at the Society of American Artists exhibition in New York in 1879, not because of its technique but for its indelicate subject matter and its gory graphic detail of a surgery in progress. Then the Pennsylvania Academy of the Fine Arts ignored the painting—it had returned to Philadelphia as part of the Society of American Artists exhibition.[5] Jefferson Medical College, out of deference to Gross and his long history with the institution, reluctantly purchased it for two hundred dollars in 1878; today the painting is worth millions and is one of the most celebrated paintings of American Realism.[6] In 1982 the Jefferson Medical College established the Eakins Gallery to showcase the painting along with portraits by Eakins of Dr. Benjamin Howard Rand (1874) and Dr. William Smith Forbes (1905).

The composition of Eakins's *The Gross Clinic* owes a debt to Velásquez's famous painting *Las Meninas (The Maids of Honor)*, completed in 1656, now in the Prado Museum in Madrid. To the left of the painting appears Velasquez himself, palette in his left hand, brush in his right. The central grouping contains recognizable court figures, the Infanta Doña Margarita, and a dwarf kept at court for amusement.[7] In the background stands Don José Nieto, the Queen's Aposentador, in the doorway, right arm extended, pointing us back to Velasquez.

In *The Gross Clinic,* Dr. Gross stands similarly positioned to the left, his scalpel replacing Velasquez's brush as the apparatus defining his role. We have another important grouping of individuals, and we also have a figure in the doorway in the background, arm extended, directing us back to the central figure. Art critic Elizabeth Johns succinctly describes the painting:

> For Gross's portrait, Eakins joined an elaborate setting and carefully selected details to give full meaning to Gross's work as a surgeon. The details are rich indeed. At the focal point of the painting, Gross holds in his right hand a blood-covered scalpel; he has just turned away from his patient and surgical assistants in order to lecture to his students in the amphitheater. The young patient lies on his right side, his knees pulled up near Gross. His head is at the far end of the table under the anesthesia-soaked gauze, his sock-clad feet at the near end; a long

incision has been made in his left thigh from which Dr. Gross is about to remove a piece of dead bone.[8]

Gross pioneered research into osteomyelitis, the condition depicted in this surgical procedure. Gross and the others appear in normal street clothes; at this time surgeons had not yet recognized the necessity of sterilizing the surgical theatre and maintaining an antiseptic environment during operations. The secondary figures are actual people whom Osler and Eakins knew, not merely representations of surgical assistants:

> An anesthesiologist and a team of four surgeons, one of whom is obscured behind the figure of Gross, assist in the surgery. The anesthesiologist, Dr. Joseph W. Hearn, presides over the administration of chloroform; on the middle right the intense figure of Dr. James M. Barton, Gross's chief of clinic, bends to his task of absorbing bleeding in the interior of the incision; and in the lower right Dr. Daniel Appel, a new graduate of Jefferson Medical College, holds a retractor in his right hand to secure one side of the incision, while in his other hand he holds an instrument ready for Gross. At the lower left of the table is Dr. Charles S. Briggs, who grips the young man's legs to keep them in position during the surgery; and, obscured behind Dr. Gross, at the upper left side of the table, another member of the assisting team holds a second retractor.[9]

Near Dr. Gross is the figure of a woman, the young patient's mother, whose face is turned away in horror and whose hands recoil at the sight of her son's blood on the scalpel. Her presence in the operating room, strangely curious to us today, and the detail of the patient's cheap homespun socks indicate that her son was a charity patient. The law at that time required that a member of the family be present to prevent the doctors from engaging in unnecessary surgical experimentation. Above her, in the first row of the amphitheatre, is Dr. Franklin West, who records Dr. Gross's narrative of the surgical process. Other individuals can be identified. Curiously, Eakins included the orderly of the college, Hughey O'Donnell, who had no function in the operation; his job was to clean up afterwards. Next to him stands Dr. Samuel W. Gross, Gross's son.

Samuel W. Gross (1837–1889), son of the principal subject of the portrait, was happily married to Grace Linzee Revere for thirteen years, beginning in 1876; they had no children. The Philadelphia medical community watched with approval as young Sam built a reputation for his research on tumors that might have equaled his father's had he not contracted pneumonia. Osler and three other highly qualified doctors treated Sam, but he died on 16 April 1889.[10] Three years later in 1892, Osler married Gross's widow.

Eakins composed his picture of Gross as a *portrait d'apparat*, a form of painting that includes objects that identify the subject with his profession. Most of Eakins's portraits of members of the Philadelphia medical community place apparati or defining objects in the pictures. His portrait of Dr. Benjamin Howard Rand (1874), a professor of chemistry at Jefferson Medical College, is cluttered with professional objects, including a compound microscope, a beam balance, and a rack of test tubes. We see the same inclusion of books, papers, and mechanical devices in Eakins's portraits of Dr. John H. Brinton (1876), Dr. William D. Marks (1886), and Dr. Horatio C. Wood (1890). All of these sitters were friends and colleagues of Osler, especially Wood who visited Montreal in 1884 expressly for the purpose of recruiting Osler away from McGill University to the University of Pennsylvania.

THE AGNEW CLINIC

When Dr. D. Hayes Agnew retired from the University of Pennsylvania medical school in 1889, the students and faculty wanted to honor him. A committee that included Osler's good friends Dr. S. Weir Mitchell and Dr. Samuel W. Gross (in the final year of his life), for some reason, chose Bernard Uhle to paint Agnew's portrait, now owned by the College of Physicians of Philadelphia. This is certainly a commendable portrait, but one could guess that Agnew could just as easily be a bank president, a minister, or a city councilman for all this portrait reveals. Osler, however, served on a different committee along with Dr. James Tyson, professor of pathology (known as "Urinary Jimmy"[11]), who had been instrumental in bringing Osler to Philadelphia, Dr. J. William White, and student representatives of each class at the University of Pennsylvania medical school. Despite the uproar over *The Gross Clinic,* Osler guided this committee to commission an Eakins painting.

Eakins's principal figure in *The Agnew Clinic*—like his counterpart in *The Gross Clinic*—a bloody scalpel in his hand, backs away from the operating table momentarily to explain the procedure, this time a mastectomy, to his students. Dr. Ellwood R. Kirby administers the anesthetic; Dr. J. William White (of the portrait selection committee), wearing glasses, wields a scalpel as chief assistant, and the nurse, Miss Clymer, stands behind Dr. Joseph Leidy Jr. who holds the patient steady. Just to the right of Miss Clymer is Dr. Fred H. Milliken, who is whispering to Eakins, who often depicted himself in his paintings (see *Max Schmitt in a Single Scull* or *The Swimming Hole*).

Seated in the gallery directly above Miss Clymer, with his chin in his hand, appears Dr. Nathan M. Baker who assisted Osler in caring for Walt Whitman. Osler, S. Weir Mitchell and others paid Baker to act as Whitman's nurse during Baker's medical school years. Baker signed as witness Whitman's last will on 29 June 1888 when death appeared imminent, but this will was superceded by others when he survived the crisis. Osler delivered the commencement address at Baker's graduation on 1 May 1889, the date on which the students presented *The Agnew Clinic* to their beloved teacher. Osler urged the young doctors to cultivate the qualities of imperturbability and equanimity. This signature address, "Aequanimitas," was later published as the lead essay in his esteemed collection of the same name, and Osler chose "Aequanimitas" as the motto for his coat of arms when he was created baronet in 1911.

Another figure in *The Agnew Clinic,* Dr. Joseph Leidy Jr. (more accurately, Joseph Leidy II) was the nephew of Dr. Joseph Leidy, one of Osler's closest older friends. Joseph Leidy Jr. liked Eakins's work *The Agnew Clinic* enough to commission Eakins to paint his portrait in 1890. Osler corresponded with the younger Joseph Leidy as late as 1916.[12]

One of the most interesting secondary figures in *The Agnew Clinic* is Dr. J. William White (also on the Agnew portrait selection committee), a great friend of Osler with links to Eakins, the writer Henry James, and the artist John Singer Sargent, who painted Osler's portrait. While Osler was in Oxford, White was a frequent visitor, and the two corresponded often. White introduced Eakins to Sargent when the latter stayed at White's home while completing a portrait of Mrs. Joseph Widener of Philadelphia.[13]

In 1905, White visited the London studio of his friend Sargent to watch him paint *The Four Doctors*, depicting the founding fathers of the Johns Hopkins Medical School:

W. H. Welch, W. S. Halsted, H. A. Kelly, and Osler. Osler alone holds an apparatus, a quill pen, a tribute to his skills and accomplishments as an author.

Though they liked and respected each other, Thomas Eakins and John Singer Sargent did not belong to the same social set. When a Philadelphia matron asked Sargent to suggest a dinner guest for one of her parties, he replied, "There's Eakins, for instance." She asked, "Who's Eakins?"[14] While Eakins painted members of the Philadelphia medical community for moderate fees, Sargent amassed a fortune by painting the likes of industrialist John D. Rockefeller, influential politician Henry Cabot Lodge, powerful journalist Joseph Pulitzer,[15] and, of course, Osler and the other distinguished leaders of the Johns Hopkins medical school.

Eakins and Sargent had markedly different styles. In his portraits Sargent improved his sitters' appearances, banishing age lines and smoothing furrowed brows. Eakins, on the other hand, often displeased his sitters by portraying them realistically; one of his subjects, Osler's friend Dr. Jacob M. Da Costa, furiously demanded in 1891 that Eakins destroy his portrait of him.[16] Both Gross and Agnew initially disapproved of the display of blood in their portraits.[17] But Eakins's realism, grounded in his scientific study of anatomy, defines his peculiarly American form of art, while Sargent's style is more typically European.[18]

CONCLUSION

There is no portrait of Osler by Eakins.[19] Why, given their mutual friendships and other associations, didn't Eakins paint Osler's portrait? Several reasons come to mind. In 1889, when he commissioned Eakins for the *Agnew Clinic*, Osler was leaving Philadelphia for the Johns Hopkins. While Osler was a beloved member of the faculty at the University of

Pennsylvania, he had been there only five years, and he had not rendered the lifetime of service to his profession or an institution as had Gross and Agnew, so he was not a candidate for a commemorative portrait. Second, Osler had not yet written his *The Principles and Practice of Medicine* (1892) which would establish his reputation worldwide. And when that masterwork appeared, Osler was not available to sit for Eakins. (Even the Johns Hopkins had to arrange for Sargent to paint *The Four Doctors* in London, not Baltimore, in 1905.)

If a portrait of Osler by Eakins existed today, it would no doubt be a treasure of inestimable worth, perhaps equaling in market value Eakins's portrait of Walt Whitman. But we do have the record of their friendship, and now we know that Osler had a connection to two of Eakins's most famous and controversial portraits.

While Osler's life is a model of decorum, he had his irreverent side, and he shared Eakins's zest for life. Osler would certainly have enjoyed hearing the story that at the Pennsylvania Academy of the Fine Arts in 1886, in order to demonstrate an anatomical principle concerning a leg muscle, Eakins removed the loincloth from a male model with women students in the class.[20] For Eakins this was a simple teaching demonstration, but for some students and administrators it was a scandalous and intolerable display, and Eakins was forced to resign. Years later, in 1904, when his reputation had grown, appropriate to his artistic talent, the same Pennsylvania Academy of Fine Arts presented Eakins with its Temple Gold Medal. The sixty-year-old artist arrived at the ceremony on his bicycle and received the medal with these words: "I think you've got a heap of impudence to give me a medal." He then pedaled directly to the United States Mint and exchanged the medal for cash.[21]

NOTES

[1] Fairfield Porter, *Thomas Eakins* (New York: George Braziller, Inc., 1959), 13.
[2] Elizabeth Johns, *Thomas Eakins: the Heroism of Modern Life* (Princeton: Princeton University Press, 1983), 55.
[3] Michael Fried, *Realism, Writing, Disfiguration: On Thomas Eakins and Stephen Crane* (Chicago: The University of Chicago Press, 1987), 3.
[4] Charles Frankenberger, "The Collection of Portraits Belonging to the College," *The Jeffersonian* 27 (1915): 5.
[5] Fried, 6.
[6] David E. Shi selected *The Gross Clinic* for the cover art for his book, *Facing Facts: Realism in American Thought and Culture, 1850–1920* (New York: Oxford University Press, 1995).
[7] See Betty M. Adelson, *The Lives of Dwarfs: Their Journey from Public Curiosity toward Social Liberation* (New Brunswick, NJ: Rutgers University Press, 2005).
[8] Johns, 47–48.
[9] Johns, 48.
[10] Frederick B. Wagner, Jr., *The Twilight Years of Lady Osler: Letters of a Doctor's Wife* (Canton, MA: Science History Publications, 1985), 136–37.
[11] Michael Bliss, *William Osler: A Life in Medicine* (New York: Oxford University Press, 1999), 129.
[12] Harvey Cushing, *The Life of Sir William Osler* (New York: The Clarendon Press, 1925), 1:244–45.
[13] Donelson F. Hoopes, *Eakins Watercolors* (New York: Watson–Guptill, 1971), 20.
[14] Porter, 23.
[15] Johns, 156n.
[16] Johns, 165.
[17] Porter, 23.
[18] Rachel Braverman, "Philadelphia's Unknown Master," *History Today* (October 1993): 2.
[19] See Alex Sakula, *The Portraiture of Sir William Osler* (London: The Royal Society of Medicine, 1991) for illustrations of all the representations of Osler, painting, sketches, stamps, busts, and plaques.

[20]Porter, 22.

[21]Darrel Sewell, "Self Portrait," in *Thomas Eakins (1844–1916) and the Heart of American Life,* ed. John Wilmerding (London: The National Portrait Gallery, 1994), 156.

CHAPTER THREE
Osler and Mark Twain

OSLER ENJOYED A STRONG PERSONAL FRIENDSHIP not only with America's greatest poet, Walt Whitman, but also with America's greatest writer, Mark Twain (1835–1910). Osler and Mark Twain knew each other through a variety of events, locations, and circumstances, and the two have some interesting parallels. They both admired the writings of Dr. John Brown of Edinburgh, Scotland. They spent time together at Oxford in 1907 when Mark Twain received an honorary degree. And although neither Osler nor Twain had grandchildren, they both were unusually devoted to young girls who served as surrogate granddaughters.

Osler and Mark Twain first met in 1881 in Montreal. Mark Twain had been in Canada for two weeks to establish residency in order to protect the copyright of his new book *The Prince and the Pauper*. About one hundred prominent gentlemen of the city gave a banquet in Mark Twain's honor at the Windsor Hotel on 8 December. Attendees included political figures such as members of Parliament, the American Consul-General, the Poet Laureate of Canada, businessmen, civic leaders, and William Osler. The Montreal *Gazette* described the gathering as "thoroughly representative of the intellectual and commercial greatness of Canada."[1]

The Department of Agriculture and Arts denied Mark Twain's application for a Canadian copyright for his novel, claiming that his two weeks residence in Montreal did not qualify as a domicile. When he arrived back in his home in Hartford, Connecticut, Mark Twain wrote a letter to the editor of the Springfield, Massachusetts, *Republican* explaining that he was merely trying to strengthen his copyright protection: "By being in Canada (and submitting to certain legal forms) when my book issued in London I acquired both imperial and Canadian copyright."[2] Canadian and American lawyers had advised him to be in Canada on the day that his novel was published in England and a day later in the United States. English copyright covered Canada as well; thus the disapproval of the Canadian authorities did not jeopardize his protection against piracy.

Mark Twain visited Ottawa in 1883 for the same purpose of protecting his copyright for *Life on the Mississippi*. When he was preparing to publish his classic *Adventures of Huckleberry Finn,* he wrote to his nephew and publishing partner Charles L. Webster: "You want to look out for the Canadian pirates."[3] Although Mark Twain left Canada without affection for the government, he had made many friends and won many readers including Osler who made an impression on Mark Twain. In the years that followed, the two often referred to each other in their writings.

DR. JOHN BROWN

We know from Harvey Cushing's biography of Osler that in 1883 Osler read the third volume of Dr. John Brown's *Spare Hours* and immediately wrote a review of the essays for the *Medical News*, his first published book review. Dr. Brown (1810-1882) practiced medicine in Edinburgh for over forty years, and gained a considerable reputation as a writer. Among the essays in *Spare Hours* two in particular appealed to both Osler and Twain: "Rab and His Friends"(1859) and "Marjorie Fleming" (1863). "Rab and

His Friends" is a highly sentimental reminiscence by Brown of his days as a medical student, recalling a working class man who brings his sixty-year-old wife to the hospital for surgery for advanced breast cancer. They are accompanied by a huge, regal dog named Rab. Both the husband and the dog are present in the operating theater during the mastectomy. Ten days later, the patient dies, and her husband follows her to the grave soon thereafter. Rab, inconsolably grief-stricken, is put to death so that he might join his master and mistress.

"Marjorie Fleming" is the true story of a child-prodigy who lived from 1803 to 1811, a young friend of Sir Walter Scott who recognized her special genius. Marjorie died unexpectedly of measles, leaving a record of unusually witty, insightful letters and poems written with a maturity far beyond her brief eight years, eleven months.

For both Osler and Twain, Rab the dog became a symbol of enduring faithfulness and love that outlasts our allotted time on earth (and for Osler the sometimes exasperatingly ineffective medical treatments that attempt to prolong that time); Marjorie Fleming symbolized youthful feminine purity and innocence, a spiritual perfection untainted by the complexities of adulthood with which we are naturally burdened.

Mark Twain met the famous Dr. Brown in Edinburgh in August 1873 when Olivia Clemens became ill. Here is Mark Twain's account of their meeting:

> Straightway Mrs. Clemens needed a physician and I stepped around to 23 Rutland Street to see if the author of 'Rab and His Friends' was still a practicing physician. He was. He came, and for six weeks thereafter we were together every day, either in his house or in our hotel. . . . His was a sweet and winning

face—as beautiful a face as I have ever known. . . . Dr. John was beloved by everybody in Scotland.[5]

Dr. Brown's essay on Marjorie Fleming inspired Mark Twain to write late in life his own essay on her, "Marjorie Fleming, the Wonder Child," in *Harper's Bazaar* in December 1909, and he unashamedly reveals his capacity to love the little girl even though she died before he was born: "I have adored Marjorie for six-and-thirty years; I have adored her in detail, I have adored the whole of her."[6] Marjorie approaches the level of Dante's Beatrice as a symbol of Platonic love.

AT OXFORD

Osler enjoyed the company of Mark Twain at Oxford in 1907 when Twain joined his friend Rudyard Kipling (1865–1936) in receiving an honorary doctorate. Kipling lived in Brattleboro, Vermont, for four years, visiting Mark Twain in Connecticut several times. Mark Twain's influence can be seen in some of Kipling's fiction. For example, *Kim* (1901)—a story about an Irish orphan who searches India for the River of Immortality with his mentor, a Tibetan lama—has strong parallels of theme and characterization with *Adventures of Huckleberry Finn*.

At Oxford, the Oslers entertained both Mark Twain and Kipling. Mrs. Osler wrote to Mark Twain:

> My Dear Mr. Clemens,
> It will give Dr. Osler and me so much pleasure if you will take luncheon with us tomorrow at 1.15.
> Sincerely, Grace Revere Osler.

Mark Twain accepted and was delighted to see his old friend

Osler at 13 Norham Gardens. Following this visit, Osler wrote to his former patient and good friend Mabel Brewster,

> We have had such a busy summer, so many people coming & going. I sent you a paper with an account of the Encaenia [a formal academic procession] & the reception to Mark Twain and Kipling. The latter stayed with us. Such a jolly fellow, so full of fun and with an extraordinary interest in everything. Mrs. K. is very bright and we fell in love with them both. Mark Twain was most enthusiastic about Kipling. It was a delight to hear them joking together.[7]

The Oslers and the Kiplings did, in fact, hit it off and became close friends for many years. Both Mrs. Kipling, the former Caroline Balestier, daughter of a successful publisher, and Mrs. Osler, a direct descendant of Paul Revere, were Americans from prominent New England families. Ten years after Osler met Kipling at Oxford, during World War I, the two would have an unfortunate coincidence; Osler lost his son Revere, an artillery officer, in combat, and Kipling lost his son John, also killed in action while serving with the Irish Guards regiment.

Two years later, in September 1909, Osler invited Mark Twain back to Oxford, but the old writer was in poor health—he would be dead in six months—and he had to decline the invitation:

> Dear Dr. Osler:
>   I wish I could say yes, it hurts me to say the other thing, but I have said it so long, now (3 years) & so often that I am at last practically used to it, like the eels. I bound myself to say no in all cases because I found that dividing the matter up & saying yes in

some & no in the others made embarrassments for me, & I have this extraordinary peculiarity: that I don't like embarrassments. But I thank Mr. Thomas for the offered compliment, & you for forwarding it.

I hope you & Mrs. Osler will come out here in the country & see me when you are on this side. It would give me great pleasure.

With kindest regards & best wishes to you both,
Sincerely Yours,
S. L. Clemens
should like to be remembered to Mrs. & Miss Porter when you see them.

Mark Twain's mention of Miss Porter in this letter leads us into territory of Mark Twain's life that remains not fully explored. In the last five years of his life, Mark Twain enthusiastically indulged himself in an extraordinarily strong attachment to young girls.

MARK TWAIN'S ANGELFISH

Twain developed an extensive correspondence with young girls—there are at least three hundred known letters to or from him and schoolgirls at the Mark Twain Project at the University of California, Berkeley. He organized this geographically widespread group into the Aquarium Club, calling the girls his "Angelfish," and decorating his most private room at his home in Redding, Connecticut, with a gallery of their pictures. Mark Twain selected only pretty girls for his Angelfish and implored them in his letters to protect the "diamond" of their purity and innocence, a symbol that would excite a Freudian psychologist.

Mark Twain's letter to Osler opened the door to his

attempt to acquire Miss Polly Porter as one of his Angelfish, although she never became an official member of the Aquarium. He met Polly and her parents at Osler's home during his Oxford visit, and their friendship continued in America when Polly's father, a writer for the London *Times*, was posted to the United States the next year. I have found three letters from Polly to Mark Twain, one of which indicates that he took Polly to see a stage performance of *Peter Pan* in New York City.

On the way to England in 1907 to receive his Oxford degree, sailing aboard the *S. S. Minneapolis*, he met Frances Nunnally from Georgia and developed an immediate liking for her. He nicknamed her "Francesca," and she began calling him "Grandpa."[8] She was the daughter of a wealthy Atlanta businessman, J. H. Nunnally. In one of the serendipitous joys of scholarship, as I concluded a paper about Osler and Mark Twain presented at a meeting of the American Osler Society, John Carson, M.D., of La Jolla, California, told us that he had treated Frances Nunnally when she was a frail old woman in California living in what appeared to be near poverty. When he noticed a picture of Mark Twain in her room, she mumbled that she was one of his angelfish, an incoherent response that Dr. Carson dismissed as the ramblings of a confused senior citizen. Dr. Carson assumed from her apparently impecunious circumstances that she could not pay for his services and treated her as a charity patient. When she complained during a hospital stay that her room lacked an elevated toilet seat, Dr. Carson jokingly told her, "Oh, I think we could buy you one of those raised commodes for about a million dollars." To Dr. Carson's astonishment, the next day her lawyer appeared at the hospital to arrange transfer of $1,000,000 in Coca-Cola stock to the Scripps Memorial Hospital.[9]

As discussed above, Dr. John Brown's essay "Marjorie

Fleming" made a strong impression on Mark Twain, so much so that he nicknamed one of his young female correspondents, Gertrude Natkin, "Marjorie" after her. On 13 February Gertrude sent a Valentine poem that she had composed to Twain. On Valentine's Day 1906, he wrote:

> It was a very sweet Valentine, & you are a dear. But I have told you that before. You got ahead of me, but it was only because I was busy. Yesterday I bought my favorite book for you, but I fell to reading it, & became fascinated, as always before, & here it lies—unsent. It is the book of that quaint & charming & affectionate & tempestuous & remorseful little child, Marjorie Fleming.
> Doubtless you are already acquainted with it. I am incurably slow and lazy, but I will send it, sure—I certainly will. . .[10]

On 17 February 1906 she thanked him for his gift and asked him,

> May I be your little "Marjorie"? . . . I will have something nice to dream about after writing this to you. Good Night. The little girl who loves you. Gertrude[11]

From this date onward, Twain consistently called her "Marjorie." He responded three days later, "Isn't it odd, you little witch! I was already thinking of calling you that name & now you have thought of it yourself."[121] Their letters often ended with reference to the lateness of the hour and pledged that they would go immediately to bed and dream of each other; they inserted in parentheses the word "blot," their secret word for "kiss." Some of their letters sound like teenagers enjoying the silly rapture of first love. On 18 March 1906 he wrote to her,

> Aren't you dear! Aren't you the dearest child there is? To think to send me those lovely flowers, you sweet little Marjorie. Marjorie! don't get any older— I can't have it. Stay always just as you are—youth is the golden time... Good-night (blot) & sleep well, you dear little rascal."[13]

But on 8 April 1906 Gertrude Natkin made a mistake and proudly announced to Mark Twain that she would soon be sixteen. She did not know that Mark Twain severed his ties with the Angelfish when they turned sixteen (Frances Nunnally was a notable exception); he considered them beyond the age of innocence and purity. He wrote to her on her birthday:

> <u>Sixteen</u>! Ah, what has become of my little girl? I am almost afraid to send a blot, but I venture it. Bless your heart it comes within an ace of being improper! Now back you go to 14!—then there's no impropriety. Good night, sweet fourteen.[14]

The next month Mark Twain wrote her a letter, greeting her with: "Hail & Aufwiedersehen." The letter itself contains nothing of importance, but he closes the letter by saying, "Good-night & good-bye. I love you dearly, you dear little Marjorie (blot) & I'm glad you have shed those two unnecessary years (blot). SLC"[15] This was his farewell letter to her. She wrote to him pleadingly, "I hope you will love me just the same,"[16] and, in still another letter, she begged him, "Please don't love me any the less because I am sixteen. No matter how old I am in years, I shall always be your young little Marjorie as long as you wish it."[17] But, alas, she had crossed the dividing line, and his subsequent responses were short, undemonstrative telegrams or brief notes.

But, what was the reason for this attraction to these dozen or so schoolgirls, these Angelfish, who formed his Aquarium? In the last five years of his life, Mark Twain was a troubled old man, disgusted with what he called the "damned human race." His favorite daughter Susy died suddenly of meningitis in 1896, much as Marjorie Fleming died suddenly of measles in 1811. His wife, Olivia Langdon Clemens, died in 1904, near Florence, Italy. His daughter Clara married the Russian concert pianist Ossip Gabrilowitsch and moved with him to Europe. His youngest daughter Jean, who suffered from epilepsy, drowned in her bathtub on Christmas Eve 1909. He had no grandchildren, and in these final years Mark Twain was a lonely old man, who, through his letters to young girls, rediscovered the pleasures of youth. His memories of his daughters during their innocent years almost certainly were a factor that led to his preoccupation with his Angelfish.

OSLER'S ANGELFISH

Are we to condemn an old man who has no grandchildren and who writes teasing letters to young girls calling them pet names? Before forming too strong an opinion about Mark Twain, let us return to our own venerable Dr. Osler who met Susan Baker, age eight, in Paris in December 1908, coincidentally just the exact time that Mark Twain was filling his Aquarium with Angelfish. Osler would spend hours enjoying tea parties with Susan and her dolls, Rosalie, Whilhelmina, and Marguerite. Osler sometimes kept the doll Rosalie with him in his hotel room, putting her to bed according to instructions from her "mother," Susan. Osler even wrote letters to Susan assuming the persona of Rosalie.

Although his correspondence matured as Susan grew older, he still teased her about Rosalie in a letter to her written as late as 1919, the last year of his life, when he, too, apparently found solace in children following the death of his son Revere on the battlefield in France.

And what are we to think of Osler's friendship with Muriel Brock, daughter of Dr. G. Sandison Brock? Osler met her in Rome in February 1909. There he took tea with Muriel and several of her young friends, giving them ludicrous instructions on table manners, telling them "to lick each finger after eating anything sticky." Muriel became one of Osler's correspondents, and he wrote to her often, calling her "Marjorie," after Marjorie Fleming, just as Mark Twain had nicknamed Gertrude Natkin. Here is a letter to Muriel Brock from December 1909 in which Osler uses his pet name for her:

> Dear Marjorie,
> I thought your photograph so good and saucy. You looked just as if you had landed a piece of soft mushy cake in the middle of your forehead. I have been behaving so much better since I saw you, & Mrs. Osler often says how good your influence has been. No wonder your father and mother are such sweet people. I wish I could get away to Rome this winter but it is impossible. If I get my lectures ready on *Table Manners* I shall certainly come in the spring. Your affectionate friend Wm Osler. My love to those other dear sweet-behaved angels.[19]

Mark Twain had his Marjorie and his Angelfish; Osler sent his love to his "Marjorie" and her friends, the other "angels." Mark Twain and Osler, two affectionate, elderly gentlemen, assumed the role of grandfather to fill an emptiness near the end of their lives of fame and accomplishment. The somewhat suggestive nature of the letters notwithstanding, no evidence exists indicating any impropriety on the part of either man. The psychological complexities of their otherwise apparently innocent indulgence adds to the lore and mystery of both. With regard to Osler, his most recent biographer, historian Michael Bliss writes, "Using every tool of my trade. . . I could not find a cause to justify the death of Osler's reputation. He lived a magnificent, epic, important, and more than slightly saintly life."[20]

NOTES

[1] Edgar Andrew Collard, *Montreal Yesterdays* (Toronto: Longman's, 1962), 282–83.
[2] "Mark Twain Explains," *The New York Times,* 25 December 1881:3.
[3] Taylor Roberts, "Mark Twain in Toronto, Ontario, 1884–1885," *Mark Twain Journal* 36, no.2 (1998): 18.
[4] Harvey Cushing, *The Life of Sir William Osler* (London: The Clarendon Press, 1925), 1:204.
[5] Edith Salsbury, ed., *Suzy and Mark Twain Family Dialogues* (New York: Amereon House, 1965), 21.
[6] Mark Twain, "Marjorie Fleming, the Wonder Child," *Harper's Bazaar,* December 1909, reprinted in Paul Fatout, ed. *Mark Twain Speaks for Himself* (West Lafayette, IN: Purdue University Press, 1978), 233.
[7] Cushing, 2: 97.
[8] Doris Lanier, "Mark Twain's Georgia Angel Fish," *Mark Twain Journal* 24, no. 1 (1986): 6.
[9] John C. Carson, "Mark Twain's Georgia Angel-Fish Revisited," *Mark Twain Journal* 36, no. 1 (1998): 18.
[10] John Cooley, ed., *Mark Twain's Aquarium: the Samuel Clemens Angelfish Correspondence, 1905–1910* (Athens and London: The University of Georgia Press, 1991), 13.
[11] Cooley, 13–14.
[12] Cooley, 14.
[13] Cooley, 21.
[14] Cooley, 25.
[15] Cooley, 28.
[16] Cooley, 27.
[17] Cooley, 29.
[18] Cushing, 2:189.
[19] Cushing, 2:204.
[20] Michael Bliss, *William Osler: A Life in Medicine* (New York: Oxford University Press, 1999), xii–xiii.

CHAPTER FOUR

Osler and Thomas Lovell Beddoes

IN 1908, WHILE ATTENDING A CONFERENCE IN VIENNA, Osler intended to make a pilgrimage to Basel, Switzerland, to visit the grave of one of the most bizarre characters in English literature, Dr. Thomas Lovell Beddoes (1803–1849). Osler had been reading Beddoes's poetry and his long work *Death's Jest-Book* for several years before. Although circumstances intervened and Osler returned to England without making the trip to Basel, his interest in Beddoes continued for many years. Osler's inquiries to both literary and medical authorities about the strange circumstances of Beddoes' death led to a clarification of the record that had been intentionally fabricated by a noted literary scholar of that time.

A native of Bristol, England, Beddoes was the son of Thomas Beddoes (1760–1808), known as the celebrated Dr. Beddoes, a physician in Shropshire. The elder Beddoes took his M.D. degree at Oxford where he briefly served as a professor of chemistry. A friend of Dr. Erasmus Darwin, grandfather of Charles Darwin, Beddoes established in 1798 the Medical Pneumatic Institute in Bristol where he published remarkable studies and became a mentor to Humphry Davy (1778–1829) who discovered the principles of nitrous oxide (which became known as laughing gas). Davy later became mentor to Michael Faraday (1791–1867), credited with inventing electromagnetic rotation. When the elder Beddoes died, tributes from poets Robert Southey and Samuel Taylor

Coleridge were effusive.[1]

Thomas Lovell Beddoes was five years old when his father died. He entered Oxford in 1820 where his classmates regarded him as eccentric. As an undergraduate he published in 1822 a play imitative of Jacobean playwrights, *The Brides' Tragedy*. The play has received scant critical attention, but one insightful analysis describes it as "a tragedy of the female condition, of woman rendered powerless by the oppressive dictates of the male consciousness" and "a disheartening, ultimately despairing depiction of women under patriarchy."[2] Beddoes struggled with his sexual identity and, according to one critic was "by inclination if not if fact, homosexual."[3]

He took his B.A. from Oxford on 5 May 1825, and began writing his great play, *Death's Jest-Book*, his *magnum opus* that would be a work in progress for the next twenty years but never published in his lifetime. One critic praised *Death's Jest-Book* as "packed, metaphorical idiom, bristling with allusion and learning, a boisterous humor that moves deliberately into the grotesque, a sense of terror before the omnipresence of death: such is the element of the extraordinary play in the composition of which Beddoes spent the most productive years of his life."[4]

EUROPE

On 27 July 1825 he enrolled in medicine at Göttingen, Germany, where he studied for four years. Along with the traditional medical studies, Beddoes attempted "to discover physiological evidence for a doctrine of immortality,"[5] seeking to discover "with the aid of medicine the proof positive . . . of an after-existence, both in the material and immaterial nature of man."[6] Beddoes sought to unite his devotion to anatomy with discoverable truths about the human condition. Christopher Moylan writes that "the dramatist peeled away the tissue of social and personal life to reveal hidden sickness. Beddoes brought to this timeworn notion of the artist . . . an insistence that clinical anatomy is directly relevant to drama."[7] Whenever his medical studies allowed, he worked on *Death's Jest-Book,* and in 1828 he sent the manuscript to England, expecting the play to become a literary sensation. But his advisors there suggested substantial revisions to improve the characterization. Ian Jack says, "It seems clear that [Beddoes's] fascination with death was the direct result of [his] father's dissections and speculations about human anatomy and the human soul. The poet was a sort of Frankenstein, a somber and impressive manifestation of the *Zeitgeist* who seems necessary to complete the literary scene in his age."[8]

Facing the daunting task of rewriting his masterpiece, Beddoes went on a drunken binge in August 1829 that lasted over a week and landed him in trouble twice with the university police. His behavior was so excessively intolerable that the authorities reluctantly told him, on 24 August, that he had twenty-four hours to leave town.

Leaving Göttingen he settled in Würzburg in Bavaria in October 1829 and, completing his medical studies, received his M.D. degree there on 10 September 1831.[9] He lived in Europe for the rest of his life, becoming active in radical political movements, moving to Zurich, Berlin, Baden, Frankfort, and Basel. Beddoes could not overcome his predilection for getting into trouble with both academic and civic authorities; nor could he curb his bizarre personal behavior and his obsession with death.

In 1846 he took a final trip back to England, visiting his few remaining friends, and in July 1847 he returned to Frankfort, then on to Basel on 3 July 1848. On 18 July while residing at the Cigogne Hotel, he attempted suicide by opening an artery in his left leg with a razor. Whether he was interrupted in his attempted suicide, or changed his mind, or simply passed out from loss of blood and rescued, the reason he was unsuccessful is not known. After he was taken to the Town (or Citizen's) Hospital, gangrene set in and, his leg had to be amputated. Beddoes suffered a stroke and died in the Basel hospital on 26 January 1849. But the story of his death does not end with this simple chronological recital of events.

Beddoes's manuscripts and papers were bequeathed to Robert Browning, the great Victorian poet who had shown admiration for Beddoes's early work.[10] Browning could not face the task of sifting through this material, and he eventually allowed Edmund Gosse (1849-1928), one of the foremost literary critics of the day, to edit the writings. When Gosse published *The Poetical Works of Thomas Lovell Beddoes* in 1890, he created from imagination the circumstances of Beddoes's death. Gosse wrote that, following the amputation of his leg, Beddoes left his hospital room, walked to an apothecary in Basel and purchased poison, returned to his hospital room, drank the poison and completed the suicide, a final note pinned to his chest. Gosse further embellished the story by making the poison curari, obtainable only from South America. He repeated these dramatic assertions in 1894 when he published *The Letters of Thomas Lovell Beddoes*. In 1928, shortly after Gosse's death, his edition of *The Complete Works of Thomas Lovell Beddoes* was published. In this final work, having communicated with Osler, Gosse retracts, in part, the circumstances of Beddoes's death, but clings to the notion that Beddoes ingested some sort of poison to end his life.

OSLER'S LITERARY SLEUTHING

Housed in the Osler Library at McGill University, several letters indicate Osler's interest in Beddoes. Those letters

Osler and Thomas Lovell Beddoes 47

deflate the suicide by poison theory and particularly the curari version. Osler corresponded with G. Lytton Strachey (1880-1932) who became the pre-eminent literary biographer of Victorian and Edwardian figures, especially politicians and writers. His best known work is *Eminent Victorians* (1918). Edmund Gosse and Strachey intensely disliked each other, both personally and professionally. In November 1907, Strachey published in *New Quarterly* the article "The Last Elizabethan" (later collected in 1922 in *Books and Characters*). He referred to Gosse's biographical treatment of Beddoes as "fragmentary and incorrect," and sniffed that it was written in a manner that would appeal "to the hearts of subscribers to circulating libraries."[11] In this pejorative comment, Strachey undermines the credibility of his rival Gosse, sole proprietor o the Beddoes material, calling him a sensationalist.

Strachey's 1907 article prompted letters from Osler to both Gosse and Strachey. He enclosed copies of a letter by A. H. Müller, the hospital director in Basel where Beddoes died. Müller's letter to Osler was written on 15 July 1907, shortly before Strachey's article appeared. Osler had asked his German friend Dr. K. Hoffmann of Basel to make inquiries about the exact location of Beddoes's grave in preparation for his planned visit in 1908. Herr Müller's letter provides those specifics along with important details of Beddoes's death:

> With regard to the Englishman Beddow I found the following information in the hospital records:
> Admissions registry entry under 18 July 1848: Thomas Lovell Beddoes from Bristol, English gentleman of means, 42 years of age, recently established here (under terms of a board allowance to be determined and with an accompanying deposit

of 100 florins) at the Hotel Cigogne, where he opened an artery in the thigh; (in the margin) died 26 Jan. 1849.

Surgical annual report 1848 (no patient records from that period are extant): operation in October: Thomas Beddoes after severing of the *Arteria cruralis gangrene; Amputatio cruris.*[12]

Surgical annual report 1849 among the deaths: on 26 Jan. 1849 Th. L. Beddoes died of apoplexy.[13]

On 16 December 1907, Osler received from Strachey the following reply:

Dear Sir

I must thank you for your very kind letter, which interested me greatly. You must, I think, have forgotten to enclose the letter you mention, as it was not in the envelope when I opened it. I hope you may be able to send it to me, as I should be very glad to hear anything about Beddoes's grave.

Do you know anything of Beddoes as a physician? I gather from what Mr. Gosse says that none of his medical work has been published; but perhaps this is inaccurate. I cannot help thinking that he may have printed papers on medical subjects—perhaps in German periodicals. It would be interesting to know what his scientific acquirements actually were; but the question can hardly be determined by a layman!

Yours very truly,
G. L. Strachey

Osler found the misplaced copy of Müller's letter and sent it on to Strachey who, in turn, replied, not helpfully, on 16 January 1908:

Dear Sir
    I was much interested with the enclosed, which I return. I should be very glad to hear any information as to Beddoes' grave which you may subsequently obtain.
Yours truly
G. L. Strachey

Gosse replied to Osler on 27 December 1907, just the same time that Strachey corresponded:

Dear Dr. Osler
    It is very kind of you to have told me that you like my book [*The Poetical Works of Thomas Lovell Beddoes (1890)*]. It gratified me much.
    All that is known about the medical MSS. of Tho. Beddoes is what I have given 1) in the preface to my edition of the "Poems," 2) in my edition of the "Letters" and 3) in my volume called "Critical Kit-Kats."
    I would not trouble you with a reference to these sources if I were not away from England, and unable to refresh my memory. Among his posthumous papers, I was not lucky enough to find a single example of his medical work, and I cannot help believing that the translation of a Swiss treatise, which he speaks of, never found a publisher, & was lost.
    There exist, or perhaps existed, some of his papers in the possession of his family, examination of which was refused to me.
    A cousin, now I think dead, replied to my request that she thought it would be best that everything he wrote should be destroyed. He seems to have awakened extreme resentment in the breasts of his

family, who, doubtless, had nothing to thank him for.

He was such a mystificateur that I have always felt a slight doubt as to the extent of his medico-physiological researches. Did he even practice as a doctor? He said so, but one does not know.

Yours truly,
Edmund Gosse

Osler's letter to Gosse must have stated the impossibility of Beddoes's death by curari and also must have indicated that he had been in communication with Lytton Strachey, Gosse's competitor. Knowing that Osler had told Strachey of the unreliable story of death by curari, when Gosse published *The Complete Works of Thomas Lovell Beddoes* in 1928, he ameliorated the story somewhat. In the introduction to that work, Gosse comments on the matter of curari: "The late Sir William Osler, however, has pointed out that the story is impossible as curari (or kurara) is not taken internally, where it has no effect, but into the blood by a puncture, which is instantly fatal. Besides, Beddoes could not have procured this rare Indian poison in Basel."[14] Using the authority of Osler, Gosse debunks the story he initiated.

Gosse still does not progress toward stating an accurate picture of Beddoes's death. He clings to the idea that Beddoes took some sort of poison and was found dead with a note pinned to his shirt. The note purported to have been found on Beddoes's chest is not a suicide note at all; it is merely a letter to his friend and lawyer Revell Phillips in England. The letter makes no mention of any desire to end his life. He does ask Phillips to give his doctor in Basel £20 (medical care was not free), and to give a case of champagne—he specified Moet 1847—to William Minton Beddoes, Thomas's cousin.[15] Written by a bedridden patient who recently had a leg amputated and whose recovery was far from assured, this letter expresses Beddoes's gratitude for friends and family, but the note hardly bears the morbid tone of finality or defeat normally expected from one about to commit suicide. Gosse, in a footnote to this final letter, says, "This note, written in pencil, was found folded on the poet's bosom, as he lay insensible after taking poison in his bed in the Town Hospital of Basel. He died at 10 P.M. the same night." I think Gosse knew better, but Osler having died nine years earlier and therefore unable to refute Gosse's assertions, he persisted in telling a more romantic and macabre story of suicide.

But we have still further correspondence, not known to Gosse, offering substantial proof that the stories of Beddoes's death were fanciful. Osler wrote to T. P. Beddoes, the son of William Minton Beddoes, Thomas's cousin who had studied with him in Berlin. On 14 July 1915, Osler received this letter:

> Dear Sir William Osler,
> Many thanks for your letter of the 2nd. inst., with Basel records.
> Few family papers are with me in London now. Enclosed are copies of two that may interest you. [Dr.] Frey, who wrote the one, was a friend of my father, they were together in Berlin.
> As to the question of curari, there seems no foundation for it until Beddoes's *Poetical Works*, Gosse 1890, in the introduction.
> I shall greatly esteem any information you can give me as to the alleged suicide. As to the curari, I should be glad to have your views, because it is impossible to ignore the possibility that my own information is either incorrect or ill substantiated.

Considering Tennyson's "Our Doctor had called in another I never had seen him before" in the Children's Hospital, it may be desirable to refute the alleged death by curari.

                Yours sincerely
                T. P. Beddoes

T. P. Beddoes enclosed typed copies of two manuscript letters, one written on 28 January 1849 by Dr. A. Frey at Basel:

To
William Minton Beddoes Esqre.
My dear William,

    It is a sad occasion that brings me to enter into correspondence with you. Our good Thomas is no more. He died here in my presence the 26th of January in his private room in our hospital at Basel where he was retained from the month of July till now by his unlucky illness.

    I think you have been made acquainted with the circumstances that forced him to stay here. A wound on his left leg producing gangrene of the foot made necessary the amputation of the leg under the knee. At that time I was forced to be for four weeks in Paris with a patient for consultation.

    At my return home I found Thomas quite well. Appetite very good. His leg going rapidly to recovery. Since that time a lingering fever began to undermine his strength. He lost his appetite.

    In the stump increasing dolours producing at last a few particles of necrotic bone. Notwithstanding I hoped to see him go to England. I had promised to accompany him to Frankfort or farther if possible and thought the depart[ure] would be possible in March.

On the 25th he sent me back some books I had lent him, by his attendant, who took back others. An hour after that, the man went to tell me of alarming symptoms of his master. I found delirium beginning.

He wrote a letter to Mr. [Revell] Phillips [Beddoes's lawyer] and spoke of his end. I and his surgeon and physician whom he had selected himself did the best we could. An attack of apoplexy made an end. He died without suffering.

Beddoes' doctor witnessed his writing of the letter that Gosse labeled a suicide note, and the doctor was with Beddoes at the moment of death. Their was no suicide note pinned to Beddoes' chest. The second letter sent to Osler by T.P. Beddoes was written by Revell Phillips to William Beddoes from his law office on 14 February 1849, just two weeks after Thomas's death:

My dear Sir,
I had a letter dated Basel from Captain Beddoes this morning. It informs me that he had been some hours with Dr. Frey, that the Dr. gave but a melancholy account of poor Tom's last days, that he had been in no danger until the apoplexy scized him, but had been ill some days previously, that he passed his time in reading, seeing no one but his medical friends, with the exception of the clergyman who visited him regularly once a week—sometimes oftener—that he had walked but twice since the amputation—once in his room and afterwards in the corridor. He dislikcd being seen, but looked forward

to coming amongst us again in England, there to remain.

Believe me,
My dear Sir,
Yours very truly,

REVELL PHILLIPS

The official hospital records, the death certificate, letters from eyewitnesses to Beddoes's death—nothing suggests that Beddoes ever walked to the village or that he would have been capable of doing so; not a single source mentions poison of any kind and certainly not curari; not one source mentions a suicide note. These competent medical professionals were with him to the end. None noted any symptoms of poison.

CONCLUSION

Edmund Gosse created this story out of whole cloth simply to have an enticing yarn to tell in the absence of any known evidence to refute him. But the evidence is clear that Gosse embellished the circumstances of Beddoes's death for several reasons. He had the opportunity to do so by being in sole possession of all Beddoes's materials; no other scholars had his proprietorship of matters relating to Beddoes. Gosse knew that a dramatic death by poison would fit the public mystique of Beddoes as a man haunted by the macabre. Moreover, the official hospital records of Beddoes's death—should anyone ever want to see them—lay in a hospital in far away Basel, Switzerland. Who would take the time to look them up and challenge the fanciful curari story? The answer of course, is one whose intellectual curiosity, grounded in both medicine and literature, would lead him to the truth: William Osler.

A final note about Gosse and his willingness to misrepresent the truth is necessary here. Gosse and Osler's friend and colleague at Oxford, Thomas J. Wise, long a respected and meticulous literary scholar, coedited the complete works of the lyric poet Charles Algernon Swinburne (1837–1909), published between 1925 and 1927. When bibliographers discovered that Wise and his accomplice Harry Buxton Forman (a friend of Dr. Richard Maurice Bucke) had forged facsimiles of the works of Elizabeth Barrett Browning, Tennyson, and dozens of other well-known writers, misrepresenting these volumes to dealers and individuals as authentic rare and first editions, Gosse also came under suspicion. Because Gosse died in 1928 before the investigation ended, he was never deemed culpable, but he died knowing that he was a suspect in the ongoing investigation of one of the greatest literary forgeries of all time that culminated in Wise's exposure and ruin in 1934.

NOTES

[1] Richard Garnett, "Beddoes, Thomas." *The Dictionary of National Biography* (London: Humphrey Milford, 1921-22), 2: 94-95.

[2] Chad Hermann, "Daughters, Wives, and Mothers: Women's Oppression in Thomas Lovell Beddoes' *The Brides' Tragedy*," *Mount Olive Review* 6 (1992): 120.

[3] Ian Beck, "'The Body's Purpose': Browning, and So to Beddoes," *Browning Society Notes* 14,1 (1984): 3.

[4] Louis Coxe, *Enabling Acts: Selected Essays in Criticism* (Columbia, MO, and London: The University of Missouri Press, 1976), 27.

[5] John Lundin, "T. L. Beddoes at Göttengen," *Studia Neophilologica* 43 (1971): 484.

[6] H. W. Donner, "Introduction." *Plays and Poems of Thomas Lovell Beddoes* (London: Routledge and Kegan Paul Ltd., 1950), xxxvii.

[7] Christopher Moylan, "T. L. Beddoes, Romantic Medicine, and the Advent of Therapeutic Theater," *Studia Neophilologica* 63 (1991): 183–184.

[8] Ian Jack, *English Literature, 1815–1832* (Oxford: The Clarendon Press, 1963), 139.

[9] Donner, xlvi.

[10] Richard D. Altick, *The Scholar Adventurers* (New York: The Macmillan Company, 1950), 232.

[11] Lytton Strachey, "The Last Elizabethan" in *Books and Characters: French and English* (New York: Harcourt, Brace and Company, 1922), 239. This is a reprint of Strachey's 1907 article.

[12] The Latin phrases *Arteria cruralis*, artery of the leg, and *amputatio cruris*, leg amputated, resemble the word *curari*. Is it possible that a layman, coming upon the hospital records, could conclude that Beddoes dramatically killed himself by ingesting curari? The story just will not go away; a recent literary biography perpetuates Gosse's story, mentioning both the suicide note and the taking of poison. See James R. Thompson. *Thomas Lovell Beddoes* (Boston: Twayne, 1985), 8.

[13] This letter and the subsequent letters in this chapter were inserted by Osler into his copy of Edmund Gosse's edition *The Poetical*

Works of Thomas Lovell Beddoes (1890), now housed at the Osler Library, McGill University. I am grateful to Pamela Miller, Osler Librarian, and the Board of Curators of the Library for permission to reprint these letters.

[14] Edmund Gosse, ed., *The Complete Works of Thomas Lovell Beddoes* (London: The Fanfrolico Press, 1928), xxxi.

[15] Gosse, 124.

[16] Gosse, 124.

[17] Alfred, Lord Tennyson, "In the Children's Hospital," first published in *Ballads and Other Poems*, 1880. This gruesomely bathetic poem, told by a nurse, recounts a visit to the ward of a doctor who "was happier using the knife than in trying to save the limb." T. P. Beddoes's reference to the poem suggests that there are good doctors and bad doctors, and that, as a good doctor, Osler should refute Gosse's baseless story.

CHAPTER FIVE

Osler and Sarah Orne Jewett

OSLER KNEW THE NINETEENTH-CENTURY AMERICAN NOVELIST and short story writer Sarah Orne Jewett (1849–1909). He especially liked her novel *A Country Doctor* (1884), but, alas, Osler failed to understand the social and sexual theme that Jewett intended in her book. The novel depicts a country doctor modeled on Jewett's father, Dr. Theodore Jewett, but he is not the main character; Nan, his adopted daughter, wants to become a doctor against the wishes of her friends, her lover, and older women in the small community. Osler misread the book and sided with the characters who opposed Nan's dream.

Osler met Jewett through their mutual friend Annie Adams Fields, the wife of James T. Fields who elevated Ticknor and Fields from a simple bookstore in Boston to prominence among American publishers, releasing titles by Longfellow, Whittier, Lowell, Thoreau, Hawthorne and Emerson, and from England such writers as Tennyson, Browning, and Dickens.[1] Osler visited the publisher whenever he was in Boston, and he ordered scores of books from them over the years.

When James Fields died in 1881, his widow Annie (1834-1915), then forty-seven, and Jewett, not quite thirty, began what has been called a "romantic friendship." Present-day feminist literary critics agree the two formed "what used to be called a 'Boston marriage': a life-long monogamous partnership between two women. This was a fairly common social unit in the nineteenth century. By the 1890s Sarah and Annie were treated as a couple by correspondents and friends."[2]

When Jewett was seriously injured in a carriage accident in 1902, Osler, with characteristic cheer, encouraged her to be patient during her long recuperation. He also wrote to thank her for some books she sent for his collection, including one that she knew to be one of Osler's favorite books, Sir Thomas Browne's *Religio Medici*, published by Ticknor and Fields.[3]

Jewett and Osler were exact contemporaries, both being born in 1849, but they differed widely in their view of gender equality at the turn of the century. Both Osler and Jewett were in step with the times with regard to the advocacy of women's rights, but they were clearly marching in opposite directions.

OSLER ON WOMEN IN MEDICINE

As late as 1891, in his address "Doctors and Nurses" delivered to the women of the graduating class of nurses at the Johns Hopkins Hospital, Osler reinforces what he saw as the natural order of things using Darwinian terms: "In the gradual division of labour, by which civilization has emerged from barbarism, the doctor and the nurse have been evolved, as useful accessories in the incessant warfare in which man is engaged."[4] For Osler and his generation, the message he wanted to convey was clear: doctors should be men, nurses women.

In December 1892, Miss Mary E. Garrett, heiress to the Baltimore & Ohio Railroad fortune and a friend of Jewett, offered $300,000 of the $500,000 necessary to open the Johns Hopkins Medical School, but she attached several conditions to her beneficence: "that women be admitted to the school on the same basis as men; that the main building of the new medical school be designated the Women's Memorial Fund Building; and that a lay committee of six women be appointed to supervise the extra-curricular affairs of the women students."[5] Privately Osler deplored these conditions. His colleague W. H. Welch said unequivocally that

> Neither Osler nor I signed the petition to the Trustees for accepting these conditions, and we sympathized with the fruitless efforts of Mr. [D.C.] Gilman [president of The Johns Hopkins University] to induce Miss Garrett to make certain comparatively slight, verbal alterations in the terms of the gift, the main change which we desired being the substitution of "equal" or "equivalent" for "same" in specifying the terms for admission of training of women and men students, but she would not budge. Still, we were so eager to start the school that we were glad that the Trustees accepted the gift.[6]

The first class of eighteen medical students entered The Johns Hopkins Medical School in the autumn of 1893; of these three were women.[7] At the end of the first year, Osler addressed the Harvard Medical Alumni Association and in a light-hearted fashion pointed out that his new school differed from Harvard's in an important way—co-education; Harvard had not yet admitted women to the medical school. He satirically told his all-male audience

> Now, while on principle I am opposed to co-education... I was warmly in favour of it particularly when the ladies came forward with half a million

dollars.... When you go against nature, you fail utterly. I come here to-day with sorrow at my heart to tell you that co-education has proved an absolute failure... When I tell you that 33 1/3% of the lady students admitted to the first year of the Medical Faculty of the Johns Hopkins University are, at the end of one short session, to be married, then you will understand why I say that co-education is a failure. If we lose 33 1/3% at the end of the first session where will the class of lady students be at the end of the fourth? In all other respects co-education is a great success.[8]

Of course, Osler was talking about only one student when he playfully cited the 33 1/3%, but humor can sometimes mask emotions such as resentment and bitterness. The Harvard Medical School did not admit women until 1945, and in the final year of the twentieth-century, in the class that completed its first year at the Harvard Medical School, 45% were women.[9]

Osler was not exceptional in his view of the role of women. According to the *Canadian Encyclopedia*, "most 19th-century Canadians, women as well as men, believed that the sexes had been assigned to 'separate spheres' by natural and divine laws that overrode mere man-made laws."[10] Remember Osler's words: "When you go against nature you utterly fail." The first woman in the United States to receive a medical degree was Elizabeth Blackwell from the Medical Institution of Geneva, New York, on 23 January 1849, seven months before Osler's birth. According to information supplied by the research division of the Canadian Medical Association, the first woman to practice medicine was Emily Howard Stowe (1831-1903). No Canadian college would accept a woman medical student, so she enrolled at the New

York Medical College for Women and graduated in 1867, but the Canadian officials would not license her until 1880.[11] Her daughter Ann Augusta Stowe-Gullen was the first Canadian woman awarded an M.D. degree in 1883 from the Toronto School of Medicine. Women such as Elizabeth Blackwell, Emily Stowe, and her daughter Ann Augusta who became physicians often became involved with the suffragist movement in the United States and Canada. For example, Anna Howard Shaw who earned her M.D. degree from Boston College in 1904 became president of the National American Woman's Suffrage Association,[12] a group founded by Elizabeth Cady Stanton and Susan B. Anthony.

This was a time of great change in both the United States and Canada as women sought the right to earn wages, to vote through participation in suffrage movements, as they established women's colleges, and, especially, as they sought to enter the medical profession. But even after women gained admission to and graduated from medical colleges, they often were relegated to staff positions in women's hospitals or women's insane asylums[13] or found work exclusively in obstetrics and midwifery.[14]

JEWETT AND THE WOMEN'S MOVEMENT

Sarah Orne Jewett was just one of many women writers who used her talent to promote women's rights, finding especially convenient the plot situation of having a bright female protagonist desiring to become a physician. Jewett admired Harriet Beecher Stowe (1811–1896), best-known for *Uncle Tom's Cabin* (1852) and probably took some cues from Stowe's novel *My Wife and I* (1871). The protagonist Caroline is brighter than her cousin Harry and helps him with his algebra. As Harry prepares to travel to Europe, she tells him that she wants the same freedom to venture out on her own, but he tells her she should be satisfied because she has beauty and talent, all that a woman needs for a happy life.[15] She asks her Uncle Jacob to pay for her to go to medical school, but he refuses to take her seriously. She finally does go to Paris for medical study.

Another famous woman writer of this time, Louisa May Alcott (1832–1888), became active in reform movements such as temperance and woman's suffrage. Jo, the protagonist of *Little Women* (1868) has an androgynous name. Alcott wrote about a tomboy heroine Nan in *Little Men* (1871) and *Jo's Boys* (1886). Nan comes to understand that in choosing to be a doctor, she must forego marriage.[16]

In 1884, Sarah Orne Jewett published her first novel, *A Country Doctor,* and perhaps unconsciously borrows the name Nan from Alcott for her central figure, Nan Prince, whose last name is a masculine title. Adopted by a childless widower Dr. John Leslie, Nan accompanies him on his rounds in the fictional Oldfields, Maine, just as Jewett accompanied her father Dr. Theodore Jewett in and around South Berwick. When Nan decides that she wants to become a physician, Dr. Leslie is proud of her and encourages her, but almost all the older women in Oldfields and the nearby coastal town of Dunport warn her against it. The name Oldfields suggests an old-fashioned, outmoded way of thinking; or, Jewett could be playing off the name of Annie Field's deceased husband. Dunport suggests dullness, a dun-colored, monochromatic drabness. Nan disturbs these sleepy, comfortable communities with her aspirations to become a doctor.

When Dr. Leslie tells Mrs. Graham, the matriarch of Oldfields, that he intends to assist Nan with her plans to study medicine, astonishment and consternation ensue, complete with a sight gag:

"Dear, dear!" said the hostess, leaning forward so suddenly that she knocked two or three books from the corner of the table, and feeling very much excited. "John Leslie, I can't believe it!"[17]

And in a chapter entitled "A Serious Tea-Drinking," Mrs. Fraley who occupies a position of social prominence in Dunport, confronts Nan directly:

"In my time . . . it was thought proper for young women to show an interest in household affairs. When I was married it was not asked whether I was acquainted with dissecting-rooms." (208–9)

She continues:

"I warn you, my dear, that your notion about studying to be a doctor has shocked me very much indeed. I could not believe my ears—a refined girl who bears an honorable and respected name to think of being a woman doctor! If you were five years older you would never have dreamed of such a thing. It lowers the pride of all who have any affection for you." (210)

Jewett uses a romantic entanglement for didactic purposes in *A Country Doctor*. The most desirable young bachelor in Dunport is handsome George Gerry, a college graduate just completing his training as a lawyer. In Dunport, in the summer following her first year at medical school, Nan and George join a group of young people for a day's picnic outing. When Nan and George separate themselves from the others to get some fresh water from a nearby farmhouse, a distraught wife welcomes them and tells them that her husband has just thrown his shoulder out in an accident. The young farmer is suffering greatly and pleads for George to go get the doctor. Nan tells the young man to lie on the floor. Then

> She quickly stooped and unbuttoned her right boot, then planted her foot on the damaged shoulder and caught up the hand and gave a quick pull, the secret of which nobody understood; but there was an unpleasant cluck as the bone went back into its socket, and a yell from the sufferer, who scrambled to his feet.
> "I'll be hanged if she ain't set it," he said, looking quite weak and very much astonished. "You're the smartest young woman I ever see." (199)

As Nan and George return to their party, George is miserable: "he felt weak and womanish, and somehow wished it had been he who could play the doctor" (200). But Nan "looked gayer and brighter than ever" (200). Later we see how much this scene distresses George:

> The truth must be confessed . . . that the episode of the lamed shoulder at the picnic party had given Mr. George Gerry great unhappiness. . . . All his manliness was at stake and his natural rights would be degraded and lost, if he could not show his power to be greater than her own. And as the days went by, every one made him more certain that he longed, more than he had ever longed for anything before, to win her love. (221)

Notice that George casts his love for Nan in terms of power and of winning her love as one wins a contest or a battle. (His last name Gerry suggests the French *guerre,* war.) But Nan has made up her mind. Against all convention, she decides that she will never marry. She says to one of Dr. Leslie's friends, a sea captain who tells her she is going "against nature,"

> "I can't tell you all my reasons for not wishing to marry... or all my reasons for wishing to go on with my plan of being a doctor; but I know I have no right to the one way of life, and a perfect one, so far as I can see, to the other. And it seems to me that it would be as sensible to ask Mr. Gerry to be a minister since he has just finished his law studies, as to ask me to be a wife instead of a physician." (237)

In the mid- to late nineteenth century, poetry and prose written by women for women fell into two broad categories: First, the sentimental stories involving affairs of the heart with the heroine ultimately successfully marrying. Nan's masculine last name, Prince, parodies the sentimental stories and suggests her dilemma: does she accede to social convention and marry her *prince* charming, or does she become a doctor and fulfill the role of prince herself.[18] The second category of women's writing sent encoded messages to a female readership, typically imploring women to stand up for themselves and not derive their identities from their husbands. In fact, writers such as Frances Osgood, Kate Chopin, Sarah Orne Jewett, and others wrote poems and stories with a theme that has come to be known as the "Adamless Eden." In the mid- to late nineteenth century, the idea emerged that women could find paradise—happiness, satisfaction, fulfillment—without a man.

A Country Doctor ends with Nan's rejection of George Gerry. She completes her medical studies and returns to

Oldfields to assist and eventually replace her aging guardian Dr. Leslie. Some women readers, expecting the traditional sentimental ending, were vastly disappointed. But these readers were not Jewett's intended audience.

OSLER'S REACTION

We know that Osler read *A Country Doctor*, but he missed the point that Jewett intended. He wrote a letter to Jewett's sister Mary on 28 February 1918 saying

> Only this week I have read the 'Country Doctor' which you so kindly sent & I am perfectly charmed with the very true & sympathetic account of a man of the highest type in the profession. As I told you I am collecting for my library the books which give an account of the social & literary side of professional life. I hope to publish a catalogue of my collection. Under the 'Country Doctor' could I state that this was a picture drawn from your Father's life & work?[19]

Certainly Dr. Leslie is an important character, but not the central character. It is Nan Prince whose fortunes we follow. It is Nan who is the title character, the "country doctor."

On one of his note cards intended to assist cataloguers of the *Bibliotheca Osleriana*, Osler wrote,

> [*A Country Doctor*] is a sketch of [Jewett's] father—a good and helpful story. . . . No pleasanter picture of the woman medical student exists than Nan, who at last married George I am sure. The ending as it is is most untrue to life.[20]

Osler and Sarah Orne Jewett

Osler's brief statement is revealing. First, he again misidentifies the protagonist as Dr. Leslie instead of Nan. Then, he describes her role in the novel as merely "pleasant." Then, unsatisfied with Nan's decision to forswear men and follow her calling, he re-writes the ending of the novel, because it is "most untrue to life."

Osler was unwilling to grant the fictional character Nan Prince the privilege of celibacy that he had granted himself for most of his life as he pursued his career. Osler did not marry until after he had completed his great work *The Principles and Practice of Medicine* in 1892 when he was almost forty-three years old with his professional reputation well-established. And when he did decide to marry, he chose the widow of a colleague, a mature woman of means who had already demonstrated her fitness to be a doctor's wife.

Most Oslerians are familiar with the famous "Latch-keyers," the young men who were Osler's interns at the Johns Hopkins, to each of whom he gave a latch-key and free access to his house at any time. But before dispatching these young men for further study at the great medical schools in Europe he also gave them a plain gold ring to wear "as a form of protection against any designing and matrimonially minded [women] they might encounter while sojourning on the Continent."[21]

NOTES

[1] David Carlin, "Sir Thomas Browne's *Religio Medici* and the Publishing House of Ticknor & Fields," *Osler Library Newsletter* (October 1998): 3–4.
[2] Josephine Donovan, *Sarah Orne Jewett* (New York: Frederick Ungar Publishing Co., Inc., 1980), 13.
[3] Carlin, 2–3.
[4] William Osler, *Aequanimitas* (Philadelphia: P. Blakiston's Son & Co., 1932), 17.
[5] Harvey Cushing, *The Life of Sir William Osler* (Oxford: The Clarendon Press, 1925), 1: 373-74.
[6] Cushing, 1: 387.
[7] Cushing, 1: 389.
[8] Cushing, 1: 398-399.
[9] Correspondence with Bill Schaller, public affairs officer, Harvard Medical School, 26 April 1999.
[10] Susan Jackel, "Women's Suffrage," in *The Canadian Encyclopedia* (Edmonton: Hurtig Publishers, 1985), 3: 1962.
[11] Carlotta Hacker, "Emily Howard Stowe," in *The Canadian Encyclopedia* (Edmonton: Hurtig Publishers, 1985), 3: 1762.
[12] Frances B. Cogan, *All-American Girl: The Ideal of Real Womanhood in Mid-Nineteenth-Century America* (Athens: University of Georgia Press, 1989), 240.
[13] Catherine Clinton, *The Other Civil War: American Women in the Nineteenth Century* (New York: Hill and Wang, 1984), 143-44.
[14] For an excellent discussion of the treatment of the female medical students by the faculty and the male students at The Johns Hopkins Medical School when Osler was there, see Michael Bliss, *William Osler: A Life in Medicine* (New York: Oxford University Press, 1999), 229–237.
[15] Ernest Earnest, *The American Eve in Fact and Fiction, 1775-1914* (Urbana: University of Illinois Press, 1974), 143.
[16] Cogan, 245.
[17] Sarah Orne Jewett, *A Country Doctor* (New York: Bantam, 1999), 104. Subsequent page citations in the text are from this edition.
[18] Jennifer Campbell, "'The Great Something Else': Women's Search

for Meaningful Work in Sarah Orne Jewett's *A Country Doctor* and Frances E. W. Harper's *Trial and Triumph*," *Colby Quarterly* 34 (June 1998): 88.

[19]Cushing, 2: 594.

[20]William Osler, *Bibliotheca Osleriana* (Kingston and Montreal: McGill-Queen's University Press, 1969), 450.

[21]Cushing, 1: 405.

CHAPTER SIX

Osler, Henry James, and Edith Wharton

CRITICS TYPICALLY DESCRIBE Edith Wharton's novels and short stories as "social observation," and many of her best works deal with high society in Old New York City where Edith Jones Wharton (1862–1937) was born into wealth and privilege. During her early years she lived in New York, Paris, Florence, Rome, and Germany. Her summers, of course, were in Newport. After her debut in 1879 in New York City, she was considered a desirable catch, and in 1885 she married Edward ("Teddy") Wharton, a handsome, good-humored *bon vivant* from an old-line Virginia family. Harvard educated, he had no profession, living instead on an allowance from his parents. Teddy loved dogs, horses, hunting, fishing, whiskey, and women. He was no match for her love of the aesthetic and the intellectual.[1]

In 1905, her novel *The House of Mirth* was the best-selling book in New York. With her money from the sale of this book she went to Europe, living away from the feckless Teddy for most of the years that followed until their divorce in 1913. She took up residence in Paris where in 1908 she began an affair with Morton Fullerton, a dashing American Expatriate living in Paris. They were introduced by their mutual friend Henry James. Fullerton, a magna cum laude graduate of Harvard, was a Paris correspondent for the London *Times*. There he covered the Dreyfus trial and wrote articles on French politics. She was dismayed to discover that Fullerton had had many affairs with both men and women. And an unfortunate episode occurred in 1909 when Fullerton was blackmailed by his French mistress.

Edith Wharton corresponded with William Osler at a time in her life when she was engulfed in personal turmoil. In 1910 she learned that her husband Teddy had squandered a substantial sum of her money buying real estate in Boston where he kept a mistress in an apartment. Also, in 1910, her affair with Fullerton had about run its course, and they parted for good in 1911.

Having been unsuccessful in both her marriage and in an affair, she thereafter developed platonic relationships with men who shared her love of literature and culture, and chief among those was novelist and short story writer Henry James (1843–1916), eighteen years older than she.

WHARTON AND JAMES

She first met the great American author James in the late 1880s at a dinner party in Paris, and they eventually became extremely close friends and confidantes. They were never lovers; James's sexual identity remains questionable, although most critics consider him at least a latent homosexual. In the Spring of 1910, Wharton assumed care of James, then living in England, who had become increasingly ill from digestive disorders brought on by depression and by the practice of Fletcherizing—chewing one's food until it is reduced virtually to liquid.

Most Oslerians already know that he examined James and prescribed a regimen for him, but letters housed in the Osler Library at McGill University reveal the part Wharton played in making this happen. James's nephew Harry, the son of the pioneering psychologist William James, came over to England from America to make initial inquiries about arranging for Osler to examine his uncle, and young Harry wrote to Wharton telling her of his plan.

James also wrote to Wharton saying, "There is a possibility of my being somehow able to see the grand Osler for a 1st class opinion."[2] She, in turn, wrote from Paris to Osler on March 7, 1910:

> Dear Professor Osler,
> My friend Mr. Henry James is very ill, and he promised me some weeks ago that if his illness were prolonged, and if in any material way I could be of service to him, he would let me know when the moment arrived.
>
> I have just had a letter from his nephew Henry James Jr., who tells me that Mr. James has just had another bad relapse, and that they are hoping, rather against hope, to build him up sufficiently to get him up to London to see you. Mr. James himself wrote me last week that he had a great wish to see you, and I wrote back at once, begging him to ask you to come down to Rye as soon as you could do so. In reply to this letter of mine, young Harry James has just written, telling me of his uncle's relapse, and of their hope to get him up to London—explaining that it would not do to ask you to come down to him because "it would be pretty formidable to Uncle Henry, who would be bothered by a sense of hospitable responsibilities which he couldn't discharge."
>
> Mr. James and I are old friends, & have talked together about his financial situation, and I think the "bother" of having you come to Rye may be complicated for him by the fear of the expense.
>
> Therefore it seems to me that the moment has come when I may act upon his promise to let me be of service to him, and relieve him of the material "bother" connected with your visit. It seems to me—as far as I can judge at this distance—

that it would be of infinite advantage to him to see you as soon as possible, and without the preliminary risk and fatigue of the journey to London; & so I write to ask if you can arrange to go down either to Ashford or to Folkestone, on the pretext of a consultation, and then run over to Rye, letting Mr. James think that you have taken him in, as it were, incidentally.

I have written Harry James that I intended to propose this to you, and that I wish to bear the expense of your visit to Mr. James. I have enjoined him not to tell his uncle anything of the proposed arrangement, but simply (should you consent) to let him learn from you that, on a given day, you will be in his neighbourhood, and will come over to see him.

I have ventured to act rather authoritatively, as you see, because Mr. James has no one near him but his young nephew, who might naturally hesitate to take the initiative in such a case—& because I feel from Mr. James's letters to me that he is profoundly discouraged, and needs to have, as soon as possible, the mental stimulus which a visit from you would give him.

   Believe me, dear Professor Osler,
    Sincerely yours,
    Edith Wharton

[P.S.] Harry James has probably told you how worried his uncle is at the thought of having to put off his play at the Repertory Theatre. This troubles him more than anything.[3]

Osler did examine James who afterwards wrote with enthusiasm to Wharton:

> This a.m. [March 14, 1910] in this place an extraordinarily reassuring & cheering & even inspiring

interview with Osler (cher grand homme who came up from Oxford apposta [especially] set the seal of my sense of being really on the way to (with a certain decent patience & care) straight & complete recovery. Osler "examined" me more thoroughly & nudely than I have ever been examined in my life.... His opinion & advice are of the highest value to me—I am exceedingly glad I saw him. But he wants me to come to him for Sunday next at Oxford (chez lui with my nephew), so as to have me for 24 hours under his close observation. I *feel* now that I am getting well—& all very quickly & almost suddenly.[4]

Of this examination, James's nephew Harry wrote,

> Osler frisked around him, jollied him, poked fun at him, told him (in Greek) that his only trouble was that he was revolving around his belly-button, &c. He prescribed a reasonable regimen and imported a nurse who was to give massage. But that involved the sort of mistake I don't believe Osler made often. It would have required constant and authoritative supervision to make my uncle stick to any regimen. Still, it was a reassuring and refreshing episode.[5]

Harry James understood that James could not be relied upon to exercise discipline with regard to food. Osler wrote to his friend Dr. J. William White on 16 May 1910, "For two or three days after my visit to him in town he seemed a different man, was able to get about, and promised to come down and stay with us; then he suddenly lapsed, and decided to go home [to Rye]."[6]

OSLER AND WHARTON

When Osler answered Edith Wharton's clandestine letter requesting that Osler examine Henry James, he answered her and made reference to her poem "Vesalius in Zante" (1902). She responded on 11 March 1910:

> Dear Dr. Osler,
> It is kind of you to write me as you have, for I sent my letter with some embarrassment, which I overcame only because no obstacle counts ... against my wish to be of some use to Mr. James.
> I am glad indeed to hear that it is possible to move him to London & that the move may have been made already; and I needn't say how grateful I should be if you could spare the time to let me know the result of your visit.
> Your allusion to Vesalius gave me great pleasure, for it was a proud moment of my life when the Librarian of Johns Hopkins wrote me, last year, that you had instructed him to unearth a copy of my verses for the library!
> They have now been put into a little volume, which I am sending you only because it contains that poem, & not with the base design of making you read the rest!—
> Please don't take the trouble to acknowledge this small offering—and accept my thanks for the address on Servetus of which you announce the approach.
> I am probably going to London on March 17th for a few days—chiefly to see Mr. James—& it would be a great pleasure if I could see you too.
> Sincerely yours
> Edith Wharton[7]

VESALIUS

Wharton's poem "Vesalius in Zante" would certainly have captured Osler's interest with its rich medical allusions and references to major figures in medical history. Andreas Vesalius (1514–64), the great sixteenth-century Flemish anatomist, studied at Louvain and Paris and obtained his M.D. degree from Padua, near Venice. There he transformed the medical world with the publication of his *De Humani Corporis Fabrica* (1543), overturning many of the theories of the Greek anatomist Galen (A.D. 130?–200?). The drawings in the *Fabrica* are noted for their superb excellence and accuracy.

Wharton takes the fanciful story of Vesalius's death and transforms it into a dramatic monologue—one person speaking with others present. Poets at the turn of the century often would select a historical or literary figure and create a dramatic monologue that tried to capture the thoughts of the speaker at moments of intensity. Robert Browning, for example, uses this technique in "Fra Lippo Lippi" (1855), "Andrea del Sarto" (1855), and "Caliban Upon Setebos" (1864). Vesalius's life involved political intrigue in addition to his revolutionary medical discoveries.

Vesalius, serving in the Spanish court as physician to the foreign ambassadors, heard that Fallopius, his successor in the chair of anatomy at Padua, had died, and that his old position was available if he wants it. But King Philip II of Spain was reluctant to give his permission for Vesalius to leave the country even temporarily, much less permanently. The tradition has it that when Vesalius opened up the body of a young Spanish girl before her actual death in order to observe the beating of her heart and the flow of blood, the Church authorities were outraged by this act. Vesalius asked permission to go on a pilgrimage to Jerusalem, ostensibly to atone for his sin, but actually to escape from Spain and return to Padua to resume the chair of anatomy. On his return voyage from Jerusalem, Vesalius died on the island of Zante, a Venetian possession off the Grecian coast.

This story of the premature post-mortem has no documented basis whatsoever and is almost certainly a fanciful creation, perhaps by some of Vesalius's enemies who still held to Galen's anatomical theories. Some think Vesalius created the story himself to escape Spain, but it seems highly unlikely that any physician would create a story suggesting that he could not tell a live body from a dead one.

Wharton's poem shows us a somewhat less than totally repentant Vesalius on his deathbed in Zante, regretting some of his choices.

The poem begins with the stock metaphor that light equals knowledge and darkness equals ignorance. Here is Vesalius on his deathbed:

> Set wide the window. Let me drink the day.
> I loved light ever, light in eye and brain—
> No tapers mirrored in long palace floors,
> Nor dedicated depths of silent aisles,
> But just the common dusty wind-blown day
> That roofs earth's millions.

He says he loves original knowledge (such as his work with the *Fabrica*), knowledge akin to natural light, not artificial. He also wishes he had stayed in touch with the common person instead of selling himself out to imperial palaces.

Then Wharton has her Vesalius persona discuss the girl he allegedly murdered for the sake of science:

> The girl they brought me, pinioned hand and foot
> In catalepsy—say I should have known

> That trance had not yet darkened into death,
> And held my scalpel. Well, suppose I *knew*?
> Sum up the facts—her life against her death.
> Her life? The scum upon the pools of pleasure
> Breeds such by thousands. And her death?
> Perchance the obolus to appease the ferrying Shade,
> And waft her into immortality.
> Think what she purchased with that one heart-flutter
> That whispered its deep secret to my blade!
> For, just because her bosom fluttered still,
> It told me more than many rifled graves;
> Because I spoke too soon, she answered me,
> Her vain life ripened to this bud of death
> As the whole plant is forced into one flower,
> All her blank past a scroll on which God wrote
> His word of healing—so that the poor flesh
> Which spread death living, died to purchase life!

This is the cold voice of one too devoted to science—science at any cost. The only value of the patient's life is what it can reveal to the scientific mind. Then Vesalius talks about opportunities missed:

> When I was young in Venice, years ago,
> I walked the hospice with a Spanish monk,
> A solitary cloistered in high thoughts,
> The great Loyola, whom I reckoned then
> A mere refurbisher of faded creeds. . .

Ignatius Loyola (1491–1556), indeed a contemporary of Vesalius, founded the Jesuit order, that robust branch of Roman Catholicism that spread into the New World and Asia. Wharton's Vesalius looked down on Loyola in the old days, but now he asks,

> For who rules now? The twilight-flitting monk,
> Or I, that took the morning like an Alp?
> He held his own, I let mine slip from me,
> The birthright that no sovereign can restore;
> And so ironic Time beholds us now
> Master and slave—he lord of half the earth,
> I ousted from my narrow heritage.

Loyola took Catholicism, gave it his own originality and power, and spread that religion to half the earth. Vesalius, having made pathbreaking discoveries and having achieved fame, forsook further research and teaching for the comfortable, lavish life at court while his successor at Padua, Fallopius, stayed the course and continued to extend the knowledge of anatomy.

Vesalius speaks about the necessity for scholars to improve on the theories of those who precede them, and he remembers the joy of scholarly competition:

> The gods may give anew, but not restore;
> And though I think that, in my chair again,
> I might have argued my supplanters wrong
> In this or that—this Cesalpinus, say,
> With all his hot-foot blundering in the dark,
> Fabricius, with his over-cautious clutch
> On Galen (systole and diastole
> Of Truth's mysterious heart!)—yet, other ways,
> It may be that this dying serves the cause.
> For Truth stays not to build her monument
> For this or that co-operating hand,
> But props it with her servants' failures. . .

Later in the poem he imagines that he can speak from

his deathbed to colleagues and predecessors about the importance of adding to the body of medical scholarship; Osler would have appreciated this particular passage:

> Truth is many-tongued.
> What one man failed to speak, another finds
> Another word for. May not all converge
> In some vast utterance, of which you and I,
> Fallopius, were but halting syllables?
> So knowledge come, no matter how it comes!
> No matter whence the light falls, so it fall!
> Truth's way, not mine—that I, whose service failed
> In action, yet may make amends in praise.
> Fabricius, Cesalpinus, say your word,
> Not yours, or mine, but Truth's, as you receive it!
> You miss a point I saw? See others, then!
> You misread my meaning? Yet expound your own!
> Obscure one space I cleared? The sky is wide,
> And you may yet uncover other stars.

Finally, Wharton concludes her poem by returning to the metaphor of light and darkness, candles and mirrors:

> For thus I read the meaning of this end:
> There are two ways of spreading light; to be
> The candle or the mirror that reflects it.
> I let my wick burn out—there yet remains
> To spread an answering surface to the flame
> That others kindle.
>   Turn me in my bed.
> The window darkens as the hours swing round;
> But yonder look, the other casement glows!
> Let me face westward as my sun goes down.

Although Edith Wharton took poetic license in interpreting the life and death of Vesalius, Osler nevertheless liked the way she captured the voice of a physician—or any professional—who, reaching the end of life, looks back on his successes and failures. When Osler first read this poem in 1902, he had not yet departed for Oxford and the Regius professorship, had not received his baronetcy. Ahead of him lay years of influencing and inspiring students and colleagues to seek the Truth. On his death bed in 1919, at the end of a lifetime of sustained success, Osler in Oxford surpassed Vesalius in Zante.

NOTES

[1] For biographical material relating to Edith Wharton I have relied upon Eleanor Dwight, *Edith Wharton: An Extraordinary Life* (New York: Harry N. Abrams, Inc., 1994).

[2] Henry James and Edith Wharton, *Henry James and Edith Wharton: Letters, 1900–1915,* ed. Lyall H. Powers (New York: Scribner's, 1990), 150.

[3] Faith Wallis and Blake Gopnik, "Finding Osler's Letters in the Osler Library: A Preliminary Report and Some Discoveries," *Osler Library Newsletter* (Feb. 1988): 3.

[4] James and Wharton, 152–53.

[5] Harvey Cushing, *The Life of Sir William Osler* (New York: The Clarendon Press, 1925), 2:219n.

[6] Cushing, 218–219.

[7] Wallis and Gopnik, 3.

VESALIUS IN ZANTE
(1564)

BY EDITH WHARTON
North American Review, 175 (Nov. 1902): 625-31

Set wide the window. Let me drink the day.
I loved light ever, light in eye and brain—
No tapers mirrored in long palace floors,
Nor dedicated depths of silent aisles,
But just the common dusty wind-blown day
That roofs earth's millions.
 O, too long I walked
In that thrice-sifted air that princes breathe,
Nor felt the heaven-wide jostling of the winds
And all the ancient outlawry of earth!
Now let me breathe and see.
 This pilgrimage
They call a penance—let them call it that!
I set my face to the East to shrive my soul
Of mortal sin? So be it. If my blade
Once questioned living flesh, if once I tore
The pages of the Book in opening it,
See what the torn page yielded ere the light
Had paled its buried characters—and judge!

The girl they brought me, pinioned hand and foot
In catalepsy—say I should have known
That trance had not yet darkened into death,
And held by scalpel. Well, suppose I *knew?*
Sum up the facts—her life against her death.
Her life? The scum upon the pools of pleasure
Breeds such by thousands. And her death? Perchance
The obolus to appease the ferrying Shade,
And waft her into immortality.
Think what she purchased with that one heart-flutter
That whispered its deep secret to my blade!
For, just because her bosom fluttered still,

It told me more than many rifled graves;
Because I spoke too soon, she answered me,
Her vain life ripened to this bud of death
As the whole plant is forced into one flower,
All her blank past a scroll on which God wrote
His word of healing—so that the poor flesh,
Which spread death living, died to purchase life!

Ah, no! The sin I sinned by was mine, not theirs.
Not *that* they sent me forth to wash away—
None of their tariffed frailties, but a deed
So far beyond their grasp of good or ill
That, set to weigh it in the Church's balance,
Scarce would they know which scale to cast it in.
But I, I know. I sinned against my will,
Myself, my soul—the God within the breast:
Can any penance wash such sacrilege?

When I was young in Venice, years ago,
I walked the hospice with a Spanish monk,
A solitary cloistered in high thoughts,
The great Loyola, whom I reckoned then
A mere refurbisher of faded creeds,
Expert to edge anew the arms of faith,
As who should say, a Galenist, resolved
To hold the walls of dogma against fact,
Experience, insight, his own self, if need be!
Ah, how I pitied him, mine own eyes set
Straight in the level beams of Truth, who groped
In error's old deserted catacombs
And lit his tapers upon empty graves!
Ay, but he held his own, the monk—more man
Than any laurelled cripple of the wars,
Charles's spent shafts; for what he willed he willed,
As those do that forerun the wheels of fate,
Not take their dust—that force the virgin hours,
Hew life into the likeness of themselves
And wrest the stars from their concurrences.
So firm his mould; but mine the ductile soul

That wears the livery of circumstance
And hangs obsequious on its suzerains's eye.
For who rules now? The twilight-flitting monk,
Or I, that took the morning like an Alp?
He held his own, I let mine slip from me,
The birthright that no sovereign can restore;
And so ironic Time beholds us now
Master and slave—he lord of half the earth,
I ousted from my narrow heritage.

For there's the sting! My kingdom knows me not.
Breach me that folio—my usurper's title!
Fallopius reigning, *vice*—nay, not so:
Successor, not usurper. I am dead.
My throne stood empty; he was heir to it.
Ay, but who hewed his kingdom from the waste,
Cleared, inch by inch, the acres for his sowing,
Won back for man that ancient fief o' the Church,
His body? Who flung Galen from his seat,
And founded the great dynasty of truth
In error's central kingdom?
       Ask men that,
And see their answer: just a wondering stare,
To learn things were not always as they are—
The very fight forgotten with the fighter;
Already grows the moss upon my grave!
Ay, and so meet—hold fast to that, Vesalius.
They only, who re-conquer day by day
The inch of ground they camped on over-night,
Have right of foothold on this crowded earth.
I left mine own; he seized it; with it went
My name, my fame, my very self, it seems,
Till I am but the symbol of a man,
The sign-board creaking o'er an empty inn.
He names me—true! "*Oh, give the door its due
I entered by. Only, my masters, note,
Had door been none, a shoulder-thrust of mine
Had breached the crazy wall*"—he seems to say.
So meet—and yet a word of thanks, of praise,

Of recognition that the clue was found,
Seized, followed, clung to, by some hand now dust—
Had this obscured his quartering of my shield?

How the one weakness stirs again! I thought
I had done with that old thirst for gratitude
That lured me to the desert years ago.
I did my work—and was not that enough?
No; but because the idlers sneered and shrugged,
I flung aside the unfinished task, sought praise
Outside my soul's esteem, and learned too late
That victory, like God's kingdom, is within.
(Nay, let the folio rest upon my knee.
I do not feel its weight.) Ingratitude?
The hurrying traveller does not ask the name
Of him who points him on his way; and this
Fallopius sits in the mid-heart of me,
Because he keeps his eye upon the goal,
Cuts a straight furrow to the end in view,
Cares not who oped the fountain by the way,
But drinks to draw fresh courage for his journey.
That was the lesson that Ignatius taught—
The one I might have learned from him, but would not—
That we are but stray atoms on the wind,
A dancing transiency of summer eves,
Till be become one with our purpose, merged
In that vast effort of the race which makes
Mortality immortal.
                              "*He that loseth
His life shall find it*": so the Scripture runs.
But I so hugged the fleeting self in me,
So loved the lovely perishable hours,
So kissed myself to death upon their lips,
That on one pyre we perished in the end—
A grimmer bonfire than the Church e'er lit!
Yet all was well—or seemed so—till I heard
That young voice, an echo of my own,
And, like a wanderer turning to his home,
Who finds another on the hearth, and learns,

Half-dazed, that other is his actual self
In name and claim, as the whole parish swears,
So strangely, suddenly, stood dispossessed
Of that same self I had sold all to keep,
A baffled ghost that none would see or hear!
*"Vesalius? Who's Vesalius? This Fallopius
It is who dragged the Galen-idol down,
Who rent the veil of flesh and forced a way
Into the secret fortalice of life"*—
Yet it was I that bore the brunt of it!

Well, better so! Better awake and live
My last brief moment, as the man I was,
Than lapse from life's long lethargy to death
Without one conscious interval. At least
I repossess my past, am once again
No courtier med'cining the whims of kings
In muffled palace-chambers, but the free
Friendless Vesalius, with his back to the wall
And all the world against him. O, for that
Best gift of all, Fallopius, take my thanks—
That, and much more. At first, when Padua wrote:
"Master, Fallopius dead, resume again
The chair even he could not completely fill,
And see what usury age shall take of youth
In honors forfeited"—why, just at first,
I was quite simply credulously glad
To think the old life stood ajar for me,
Like a fond woman's unforgetting heart.
But now that death waylays me—now I know
This isle is the circumference of my days,
And I shall die here in a little while—
So also best, Fallopius!
      For I see
The gods may give anew, but not restore;
And though I think that, in my chair again,
I might have argued my supplanters wrong
In this or that—this Cesalpinus, say,
With all his hot-foot blundering in the dark,

Fabricius, with his over-cautious clutch
On Galen (systole and diastole
Of Truth's mysterious heart!)—yet, other ways,
It may be that this dying serves the cause.
For Truth stays not to build her monument
For this or that co-operating hand,
But props it with her servants' failures—nay,
Cements its courses with their blood and brains,
A living substance that shall clinch her walls
Against the assaults of time. Already, see,
Her scaffold rises on my hidden toil,
I but the accepted premiss whence must spring
The airy structure of her argument;
Nor could the bricks it rests on serve to build
The crowning finials. I abide her law:
A different substance for a different end—
Content to know I hold the building up;
Though men, agape at dome and pinnacles,
Guess not, the whole must crumble like a dream
But for that buried labor underneath.
Yet, Padua, I had still my word to say!
Let others say it!—Ah, but will they guess
Just the one word—? Nay, Truth in many-tongued.
What one man failed to speak, another finds
Another word for. May not all converge
In some vast utterance, of which you and I,
Fallopius, were but halting syllables?
So knowledge come, no matter how it comes!
No matter whence the light falls, so it fall!
Truth's way, not mine—that I, whose service failed
In action, yet may make amends in praise.
Fabricius, Cesalpinus, say your word,
Not yours, or mine, but Truth's, as you receive it!
You miss a point I saw? See others, then!
Misread my meaning? Yet expound your own!
Obscure one space I cleared? The sky is wide,
And you may yet uncover other stars.
For thus I read the meaning of this end:
There are two ways of spreading light; to be

The candle or the mirror that reflects it.
I let my wick burn out—there yet remains
To spread an answering surface to the flame
That others kindle.

Turn me in my bed.
The window darkens as the hours swing round;
But yonder, look, the other casement glows!
Let me face westward as my sun goes down.

CHAPTER SEVEN

Osler and Robert Browning

AT CHRISTMAS 1912, Osler's lifelong friend Ned Milburn sent him a copy of Robert Browning's lengthy poem "Rabbi Ben Ezra." Osler thanked his friend, saying, "Dear Ned, Thanks for the Rabbi Ben Ezra—a favorite poem of mine, the best of Browning's, I think." Osler had quoted this poem as early as twenty years before receiving the copy from Milburn, so we know that the high regard he expressed for it is genuine.

Osler enjoyed good literature and he especially liked the British writers of the early nineteenth century—Keats, Wordsworth, Shelley. But he also liked a later generation—Tennyson, Browning, even the notorious Oscar Wilde.

The poem "Rabbi Ben Ezra" is based upon the life of an actual person, Abraham-ben-Meir Aben-Ezra (ca. 1092–1167). What was it about Ben Ezra that caused Browning to compose a poem inspired by him? What attracted Osler to Browning's poem?

Recall that Robert Browning (1812–1889) and Elizabeth Barrett Browning (1806–1861) had one of the literary world's great love affairs. She was six years older than he and already an established poet when he presumed to write to her. In his first letter to her on 10 January 1845, he said, "I love your verses with all my heart, dear Miss Barrett. . . and I love you too." They had never met, but something in her poetry made him fall in love with her.

She was a semi-invalid, almost forty years old, living in her family's home on Wimpole Street in London. Her overprotective father kept all suitors at bay and discouraged Elizabeth's participation in any social activity outside the home.

When Browning asked permission to call on her and meet her personally, she would not grant it. But a steady correspondence ensued, and they fell in love through their long letters. Finally, she consented to a visit, and they fell more in love than ever. He proposed and she accepted, but her father refused to give his permission.

Then they did a most scandalous act: They eloped. Not only did they commit this madcap breach of decorum, but also they ran away to Italy. Someone said that if you could cut open Browning's heart you would find the word "Italy" engraved there. Away from gloomy London, in sunny Italy, with her devoted Browning, Elizabeth's health improved. And most miraculous of all, she was able to bear a child, a son, whom they nicknamed "Pen." Theirs was an ecstatically happy marriage until her death in 1861. Browning was to live almost thirty years longer.

When Browning wrote "Rabbi Ben Ezra" in 1864, he was fifty-two years old, not exactly antique, but mature. Having emerged from his grief over the loss of Elizabeth, he is in full voice as a poet. He adopts the persona of Rabbi Ben Ezra to express an optimistic religious view of the approach of old age and death.[1]

The actual Rabbi Ben Ezra was a Spanish Jewish thinker who was born in Toledo. The term "rabbi" means more than just "teacher"; the term is reserved for those who are qualified to interpret Jewish law. Ben Ezra traveled widely, visiting Palestine, Persia, India, Italy, France, and England. A peripatetic scholar such as Ben Ezra would visit libraries and universities, such as they were, to lecture, telling what he knew, and to hear what other scholars knew. He was well-versed in medicine, poetry, philosophy, astronomy, mathematics—almost any field of human inquiry. He was called the Admirable Doctor, and, as we know, the word *doctor* also means teacher as in *docent*. His reputation survives because his excellent commentaries on the Sacred Books survive. He died returning to Spain from Rome in 1167.

Browning scholars think that the poet has faithfully reproduced the philosophy of the actual Ben Ezra; further, they think the poem is "one of the clearest expositions of Browning's own philosophy of life."[2] By extension, then, the poem also articulates Osler's philosophy.

Many people are familiar with the opening lines but think they come from a love poem: "Grow old along with me!/ The best is yet to be." The idea of the poem is that for Ben Ezra "life is to be a continual striving after the highest, which can only be reached in so-called death. It is his belief that only in age does man begin to *know*, and that therefore it is contrary to all the idea of God's love to think that just before success the end shall come to annul the labour of so many years. Thus he feels that death is but the perfecting crisis in the life of the soul which is immortal."[3]

In other words, what sort of God would allow us to develop our knowledge and skills, to bring us to the "top of our game" and then simply let us die? Something better must follow death. Old age is not a declination of our power but a culmination. This poem is about the triumph of old age which is "an apex, a pinnacle, from which all the efforts and errors of the past can be reviewed."[4]

OSLER CITES BROWNING

Osler frequently quoted from the poem in his various

addresses to the medical community. In 1892, for instance, in "Teacher and Student," an address at the University of Minnesota on the occasion of the opening of the new medical buildings there, he said,

> My message is chiefly to you, Students of Medicine, since with the ideals entertained now your future is indissolubly bound. The choice lies open, the paths are plain before you. Always seek your own interests, make of a high and sacred calling a sordid business, regard your fellow creatures as so many tools of trade, and, if your heart's desire is for riches, they may be yours; but you will have bartered away the birthright of a noble heritage, traduced the physician's well-deserved title of the Friend of Man, and falsified the best traditions of an ancient and honourable Guild. On the other hand, I have tried to indicate some of the ideals which you may reasonably cherish. No matter though they are paradoxical in comparison with the ordinary conditions in which you work, they will have, if encouraged, an ennobling influence, even if it be for you only to say with Rabbi Ben Ezra, 'what I aspired to be and was not, comforts me.' And though this course does not necessarily bring position or renown, consistently followed it will at any rate give to your youth an exhilarating zeal and a cheerfulness which will enable you to surmount all obstacles—to your maturity a serene judgment of men and things, and that broad charity without which all else is nought—to your old age that greatest of blessings, peace of mind, a realization, maybe, of the prayer of Socrates for the beauty in the inward soul and for unity of the outer and the inner man.[5]

The full verse from which Osler quotes is stanza 7:

> For thence,—a paradox
> Which comforts while it mocks,
> Shall life succeed in that it seems to fail:
> What I aspired to be,
> And was not, comforts me:
> A brute I might have been, but would not sink i' the scale.

How can we be comforted by failing to achieve that to which we aspire? You improve yourself, you rise above the brute, Osler says to the medical students, by daring, and sometimes when you dare, you fail.

In 1894, in an address to the McGill University Medical School, "Teaching and Thinking," Osler calls upon McGill to realize the importance of research as a complement to good teaching. In particular, he urges caution in acceding to patients' growing demand for drugs. Osler said,

> It cannot be denied that we have learned more rapidly how to prevent than how to cure diseases, but with a definite outline of our ignorance we no longer live now in a fool's Paradise, and fondly imagine that in all cases we control the issues of life and death with our pills and potions. It took the profession many generations to learn that fevers ran their course, influenced very little, if at all, by drugs. . . . Of the difficulties inherent in the art not one is so serious as this which relates to the cure of disease by drugs. There is so much uncertainty and discord even among the best authorities (upon non-essentials it is true) that I always feel the force of a well-known stanza in *Rabbi Ben Ezra—*

> Now, who shall arbitrate?
> Ten men love what I hate,
> Shun what I follow, slight what I receive;
> Ten, who in ears and eyes
> Match me: we all surmise,
> They this thing, and I that: whom shall my <u>soul</u> believe?[6] (Stanza 22)

In 1903, at the centennial celebration of the New Haven Medical Association, he spoke "On the Educational Value of the Medical Society." He said,

> As the practice of medicine is not a business and can never be one, the education of the heart—the moral side of the man—must keep pace with the education of the head. Our fellow creatures cannot be dealt with as man deals in corn and coal; 'the human heart by which we live' [Wordsworth: "Intimations of Immortality"] must control our professional relations.
> After all, the personal equation has most to do with success or failure in medicine, and in the trials of life the fire which strengthens and tempers the metal of one may soften and ruin another. In his philosophy of life, the young doctor will find Rabbi Ben Ezra a better guide, with his stimulating
>
> Then, welcome each rebuff
> That turns earth's smoothness rough,
> Each sting that bids nor sit nor stand but go!
> (Stanza 6)
>
> than Omar, whose fatalism, so seductive in Fitzgerald's verses, leaves little scope for human effort.[7]

Through Browning's words, Osler tells his colleagues to take the good with the bad.

In "A Way of Life," delivered to Yale students in 1913, "he recommends developing a way of life based on established habits."[8] Remember how he urges "day-tight" compartments in one's life? He tells the Yale students, "I sometimes wonder whether or not Socrates and Plato would find the race improved. I am sure they would love to look on such a gathering as this. Make their ideal yours—the fair mind in the fair body. The one cannot be sweet and clean without the other, and you must realize, with Rabbi Ben Ezra, the great truth that flesh and soul are mutually helpful."[9] Osler refers to stanza 12, the exact lines of which read, "Let us cry 'All good things/ Are ours, nor soul helps flesh more, now, than flesh helps soul!"

And in that same address, without citing his source, Osler says, "Do not worry your brains about that bugbear Efficiency, which, sought consciously and with effort, is just one of those elusive qualities very apt to be missed. The man's college output is never to be gauged at sight; all the world's coarse thumb and finger may fail to plumb his most effective work, the casting of the mental machinery of self-education, the true preparation for a field larger than the college campus."[10]

Osler excerpted words from stanza 24 of Browning's poem:

> But all, the world's coarse thumb
> And finger failed to plumb,
> So passed in making up the main account;
> All instincts immature,
> All purposes unsure,
> That weighed not as his work, yet swelled the man's amount.

Here Browning speaks of the failure of science to account for man's worth. Science alone is not enough. Osler extends the thought that knowledge of medicine is not enough. Expand yourselves, says Osler; swell your account.

In 1910, Osler spoke to students in Edinburgh at a meeting on tuberculosis. He told them, in "Man's Redemption of Man," "From Homer to Lucian there is one refrain—the pride in the body as a whole; and in the strong conviction that 'our soul in its rose-mesh' is quite as much helped by flesh as flesh is by soul, the Greek sang his song 'For pleasant is this flesh.' The beautiful soul harmonizing with a beautiful body is as much the glorious ideal of Plato as it is the end of the education of Aristotle."[11]

Here he quotes from stanza eleven:

For pleasant is this flesh;
   Our soul, in its rose-mesh
Pulled ever to the earth, still yearns for rest;
   Would we some prize might hold
   To match those manifold
Possessions of the brute,—gain most, as we did best!

How does this stanza relate to Osler's message? He believed that the suffering of the body was being alleviated by scientific advances in medicine. As those advances continued, man could turn his attention to the redemption of his soul.

CONCLUSION

Finally, in "Aequanimitas," an address Osler gave at the University of Pennsylvania in 1889 on the occasion of his departure for The Johns Hopkins, he urges the students to develop imperturbability and equanimity: "I can but wish that you may reap the promised blessing of quietness and of assurance forever, until 'Within this life,/ Though lifted o'er its strife" [Verse 17], you may, in the growing winters, glean a little of that wisdom which is pure, peaceable, gentle, full of mercy and good fruits, without partiality and without hyposcrisy." The entire stanza merits quoting:

> So, still within this life,
> Though lifted o'er its strife,
> Let me discern, compare, pronounce at last,
>   "This rage was right i' the main,
>   That acquiescence vain:
> The Future I may face...now I have proved the Past."

Browning does not say that the gifts of youth—beautiful, healthy bodies—have no worth. But certainly Browning and Osler both urge the view that the fleshly pleasures of youth yield to the higher pleasures of old age. With old age comes knowledge and experience, experience that has learned to value failure as well as success. One of Browning's most optimistic poems, it has been described as "the noblest of modern religious poems."[12]

Osler quotes from Browning's "Rabbi Ben Ezra" in six addresses from 1889 to 1910, and doubtless he used the poem on other occasions as well. Clearly, this was, as he told his old friend Milburn, one of his favorite poems.

NOTES

[1] William Irvine and Park Honan, *The Book, the Ring, and the Poet: A Biography of Robert Browning* (New York: McGraw-Hill Book Company, 1974), 398–99.

[2] James Stephens, Edwin L. Beck, and Royall H. Snow, eds. *Victorian and Later English Poets* (New York: American Book Company, 1949), 353.

[3] Esther Phoebe Defies, *A Browning Primer* (Port Washington, NY: Kennikat Press, 1970), 68–69.

[4] Edward Dowden, *Robert Browning* (Port Washington, NY: Kennikat Press, 1970), 236.

[5] William Osler, "Teacher and Student," in *Osler's "A Way of Life" and Other Addresses, with Commentary and Annotations*, Sigeaki Hinohara and Hisae Niki, eds. (Durham, NC: Duke University Press, 2001), 123–24.

[6] Osler, "Teaching and Thinking," in *Osler's "A Way of Life,"* 180.

[7] Osler, "On the Educational Value of the Medical Society," in *Aequanimitas* (Philadelphia: P. Blakiston's Son & Co., Inc., 1932), 333–34.

[8] Osler, *Osler's "A Way of Life" and Other Addresses, with Commentary and Annotations*, 1.

[9] Osler, "A Way of Life," in *Osler's "A Way of Life,"* 11–12.

[10] Osler, "A Way of Life," in *Osler's "A Way of Life,"* 14–15.

[11] Osler, "Man's Redemption of Man," in *Osler's "A Way of Life,"* 360.

[12] Arthur Symons, *An Introduction to the Study of Browning*, 2nd ed. rev. (Port Washington, NY: Kennikat Press, 1970), 129.

RABBI BEN EZRA
(1864)
By Robert Browning

I

Grow old along with me!
The best is yet to be,
The last of life, for which the first was made:
Our times are in His hand
Who saith, "A whole I planned,
Youth shows but half; trust God: see all nor be afraid!"

II

Not that, amassing flowers,
Youth sighed "Which rose make ours,
Which lily leave and then as best recall?"
Not that, admiring stars,
It yearned "Nor Jove, nor Mars:
Mine be some figured flame which blends, transcends them all!"

III

Not for such hopes and fears
Annulling youth's brief years,
Do I remonstrate: folly wide the mark!
Rather I prize the doubt
Low kinds exist without,
Finished and finite clods, untroubled by a spark.

IV

Poor vaunt of life indeed,
Were man but formed to feed
On joy, to solely seek and find and feast:
Such feasting ended, then
As sure an end to men;
Irks care the crop-full bird? Frets doubt the maw-crammed beast?

V

Rejoice we are allied
To That which doth provide
And not partake, effect and not receive!
A spark disturbs our clod;
Nearer we hold of God
Who gives, than of His tribes that take, I must believe.

VI

Then, welcome each rebuff
That turns earth's smoothness rough,
Each sting that bids nor sit nor stand but go!
Be our joys three-parts pain!
Strive, and hold cheap the strain;
Learn, nor account the pang; dare, never grudge the throe!

VII

For thence,—a paradox
Which comforts while it mocks,—
Shall life succeed in that it seems to fail:
What I aspired to be,
And was not, comforts me:
A brute I might have been, but would not sink i' the scale.

VIII

What is he but a brute
Whose flesh as soul to suit,
Whose spirit works lest arms and legs want play?
To man, propose this test—
Thy body at its best,
How far can that project thy soul on its lone way?

IX

Yet gifts should prove their use:
I own the Past profuse
Of power each side, perfection every turn:
Eyes, ears took in their dole,
Brain treasured up the whole;
Should not the heart beat once "How good to live and learn?"

X

Not once beat "Praise be Thine!
I see the whole design,
I, who saw power, see now Love perfect too:
Perfect I call They plan:
Thanks that I was a man!
Maker, remake, complete,—I trust what Thou shalt do!"

XI

For pleasant is this flesh;
Our soul, in its rose-mesh
Pulled ever to the earth, still yearns for rest;
Would we some prize might hold
To match those manifold
Possessions of the brute,—gain most, as we did best!

XII

Let us not always say
"Spite of this flesh to-day
I strove, made head, gained ground upon the whole!"
As the bird wings and sings,
Let us cry "All good things
Are ours, nor soul helps flesh more, now, than flesh helps soul!"

XIII

  Therefore I summon age
  To grant youth's heritage,
Life's struggle having so far reached its term:
  Thence shall I pass, approved
  A man, for aye removed
From the developed brute; a god though in the germ.

XIV

  And I shall thereupon
  Take rest, ere I be gone
Once more on my adventure brave and new:
  Fearless and unperplexed,
  When I wage battle next,
What weapons to select, what armour to indue.

XV

  Youth ended, I shall try
  My gain or loss thereby;
Leave the fire ashes, what survives is gold:
  And I shall weigh the same,
  Give life its praise or blame:
Young, all lay in dispute: I shall know, being old.

XVI

  For note, when evening shuts,
  A certain moment cuts
The deed off, calls the glory from the grey:
  A whisper from the west
  Shoots—"Add this to the rest,
Take it and try its worth: here dies another day."

XVII

So, still within this life,
Though lifted o'er its strife,
Let me discern, compare, pronounce at last,
"This rage was right i' the main,
That acquiescence vain:
The Future I may face now I have proved the Past."

XVIII

For more is not reserved
To man, with soul just nerved
To act to-morrow what he learns to-day:
Here, work enough to watch
The Master work, and catch
Hints of the proper craft, tricks of the tool's true play.

XIX

As it was better, youth
Should strive, through acts uncouth,
Toward making, than repose on aught found made:
So, better, age, exempt
From strife, should know, than tempt
Further. Thou waitedst age: wait death nor be afraid!

XX

Enough now, if the Right
And Good and Infinite
Be named here, as thou callest thy hand thine own,
With knowledge absolute,
Subject to no dispute
From fools that crowded youth, nor let thee feel alone.

XXI

Be there, for once and all,
Severed great minds from small,
Announced to each his station in the Past!
Was I, the world arraigned,
Were they, my soul disdained,
Right? Let age speak the truth and give us peace at last!

XXII

Now, who shall arbitrate?
Ten men love what I hate,
Shun what I follow, slight what I receive;
Ten, who in ears and eyes
Match me: we all surmise,
They this thing, and I that: whom shall my soul believe?

XXIII

Not on the vulgar mass
Called "work," must sentence pass,
Things done, that took the eye and had the price;
O'er which, from level stand,
The low world laid its hand,
Found straightway to its mind, could value in a trice:

XXIV

But all, the world's coarse thumb
And finger failed to plumb,
So passed in making up the main account;
All instincts immature,
All purposes unsure,
That weighed not as his work, yet swelled the man's amount:

XXV

Thoughts hardly to be packed
Into a narrow act,
Fancies that broke through language and escaped;
All I could never be,
All, men ignored in me,
This, I was worth to God, whose wheel the pitcher shaped.

XXVI

Ay, note that Potter's wheel,
That metaphor! and feel
Why time spins fast, why passive lies our clay,—
Thou, to whom fools propound,
When the wine makes its round,
"Since life fleets, all is change; the Past gone, seize to-day!"

XXVII

Fool! All that is, at all,
Lasts ever, past recall;
Earth changes, but thy soul and God stand sure:
What entered into thee,
That was, is, and shall be:
Time's wheel runs back or stops: Potter and clay endure.

XXVIII

He fixed thee mid this dance
Of plastic circumstance,
This Present, thou, forsooth, wouldst fain arrest:
Machinery just meant
To give thy soul its bent,
Try thee and turn thee forth, sufficiently impressed.

XXIX

What though the earlier grooves
Which ran the laughing loves
Around thy base, no longer pause and press?
What though, about they rim,
Skull-things in order grim
Grow out, in graver mood, obey the sterner stress?

XXX

Look not thou down but up!
To uses of a cup,
The festal board, lamp's flash and trumpet's peal,
The new wine's foaming flow,
The Master's lips aglow!
Thou, heaven's consummate cup, what need'st thou with earth's wheel?

XXXI

But I need, now as then,
Thee, God, who mouldest men;
And since, not even while the whirl was worst,
Did I,—to the wheel of life
With shapes and colours rife,
Bound dizzily,—mistake my end, to slake Thy thirst:

XXXII

So, take and use Thy work:
Amend what flaws may lurk,
What strain o' the stuff, what warpings past the aim!
My times be in Thy hand!
Perfect the cup as planned!
Let age approve of youth, and death complete the same!

CHAPTER EIGHT

❦ Osler and Nathan Smith ❧

OSLER ADMIRED NATHAN SMITH (1762–1829) and praised him often in his speeches, but few medical professionals today know of his accomplishments during his lifetime and of his legacy. He inspired Osler with his vision and energy as the founder of four medical colleges in the United States. He was born in Rehobeth, Massachusetts, and spent his boyhood in Vermont. When he was about twenty-one years of age, earning his living as a farmer, he assisted Dr. Josiah Goodhue in Putney, Vermont, in tying off an artery during an amputation. This was not at all uncommon for the local country doctor to enlist the aid of whoever happened to be nearby. Smith impressed Dr. Goodhue with his dexterity and affinity for surgery. Goodhue made Smith his apprentice and took him about the countryside for three years to sharpen his skills. In 1787 Smith began his own practice without the benefit of any college training whatsoever. Goodhue enlisted the aid of a local minister to prepare young Smith for entrance to Harvard.[1]

After reading the classics and developing his writing ability, Smith entered Harvard in 1789 and received his M.B. (Bachelor of Medicine) degree in 1790, after only one year of study. Had he stayed for a second year and attended exactly the same lectures, he would have received the M.D. degree. Such was the state of medical education in the United States. After Smith attained his estimable reputation, Harvard converted his bachelor's to a doctoral degree. Following graduation he practiced medicine in the town of Cornish, New Hampshire. But he realized that he needed more formal training, and he also knew that New England was woefully in need of institutions at which young men could receive medical education. In December 1796 he traveled to Edinburgh, Glasgow, and London to study at the great medical centers there for six months. Of these three centers, Edinburgh was pre-eminent. In his picaresque novel *The Expedition of Humphrey Clinker* (1771), the Scottish writer Tobias Smollett says, "The University of Edinburgh is supplied with excellent professors in all the sciences; and the medical school, in particular, is famous all over Europe. The students of this art have the best opportunity of learning it to perfection, in all its branches." Smith did not enroll in a specific course, nor did he take a degree; he simply audited lectures on topics in which he felt deficient, especially chemistry. In London he attended "meetings of the Medical Society of London, where physicians met surgeons and apothecaries in a collegial search for knowledge."[2] He was voted a corresponding member of the Society in May 1797.

Smith returned to the United States in September 1797 and began teaching the first medical classes at Dartmouth College in November of that year. To say that Dartmouth instantaneously had a medical school is misleading. What it had was Dr. Nathan Smith, the sole professor. But to put the situation in perspective, Harvard had only three professors, and Edinburgh had only ten. He taught anecdotally and extemporaneously, a style that Osler later used in his lectures. Having labored as a country doctor, Smith brought to his classroom practical experience.

When Yale College wanted to open a medical institution in 1813, the directors prevailed upon Smith to become the first Professor of Theory and Practice of Physic and Surgery. The only other professor was Benjamin Silliman who taught Chemistry. In its official literature, Yale credits its leading faculty member with the founding of the Medical Institution and praises his innovative, practical approach to medicine and surgery.

Without severing his ties to the medical college at Yale, in 1821 Smith organized the Medical Department of Bowdoin College in Brunswick, and it became the Medical School of Maine. That institution survived one hundred years but closed its doors in 1921 because of poor financial management and the reduction of available young men as both students and professors during the years of World War I.

Still linked to Yale, Nathan Smith established a fourth medical college at the University of Vermont in Burlington in 1821 and taught there intermittently for four years. He resigned all of his professorships in 1825 and died in 1829.[3]

OSLER'S ADMIRATION

Osler acknowledged the contributions of Nathan Smith to American medical education in many speeches. In 1901, in "Medicine in the Nineteenth Century," he said

> The leading practitioners in the early years were Rush and Physick, in Philadelphia; Hosack and Mitchill, in New York; and James Jackson and John Collins Warren, in Boston. There were throughout the country, in smaller places, men of great capabilities and energy, such as Nathan Smith, the founder of the Medical Schools of Dartmouth and of Yale.[4]

Cushing quotes Osler as saying, "If I had typhoid fever and had a theosophic option as to a family physician I would choose Nathan Smith, nor would I care whether it was while he laboured in the flesh in the little town of Cornish, New Hampshire, in 1798, or after he had become the distinguished professor of Medicine in Yale."[5] This is high praise indeed for Osler to express a preference for Smith as his family physician.

In 1902, in "Some Aspects of American Medical Bibliography," Osler said,

> There should be a local pride in collecting the writings and manuscripts of the men who have made a school or a city famous. It is astonishing how much manuscript material is stowed away in old chests and desks. . . . Think of the precious letters of that noble old man, Nathan Smith, full of details about the foundations of the Dartmouth and the Yale Schools of Medicine! Valuable now (too valuable to be in private hands), what will they be 100 or 200 years hence![6]

One hundred years hence, we regard Osler with the same awe that he attributed to Smith. In 1905, when Osler delivered his farewell address in New York City as he departed for Oxford, he said,

> I have had but two ambitions in the profession: first to make of myself a good clinical physician, to be ranked with the men who have done so much for the profession of this country—to rank in the class with Nathan Smith, Bartlett, James Jackson, Bigelow, Alonzo Clark, Metcalfe, W. W. Gerhard, Draper, Pepper, DaCosta and others. The chief desire of my life has been to become a clinician of the same stamp with these great men, whose names we all revere and who did so much good work for clinical medicine.[7]

Osler's second desire was to build up great North American clinics on the British and German models. Representing for Osler the best in progressive American medical education, Nathan Smith appears at the top of his list of an American pantheon of medical notables.

SMITH'S LEGACY

Nathan Smith's sons and grandsons continued their patriarch's contributions to the medical profession in America. Smith had four sons, all of whom became physicians: David Solon Chase Hall Smith (1795–1859), M.D. Yale, 1816; Nathan Ryno Smith (1797–1877), M.D. Yale, 1820; James Morven Smith (1805–53), M.D. Yale, 1828; John Derby Smith (1812–84), M.D. University of Maryland, 1846. Of these four sons, the most accomplished was Nathan Ryno Smith who became one of the first professors of anatomy in the new Jefferson Medical College in Philadelphia where he taught Samuel D. Gross, called "the Emperor of American Surgery" (see Chapter 2). You will recall that Osler married the widow of Samuel D. Gross's son Samuel W. Gross. In 1827 Ryno accepted the chair of surgery at the University of Maryland, and he taught there for fifty years, active until his death in 1877.

Osler also recognized the contributions of Ryno Smith. In "Books and Men" delivered at the Boston Medical Library in 1901. Osler said,

> In medicine the men New England has given to the other parts of the country have been better than books. Men like Nathan R. Smith, Austin Flint, Willard Parker, Alonzo Clark, Elisha Bartlett, John D. Dalton, and others carried away from their New England homes a love of truth, a love of learning,

and above all a proper estimate of the personal character of the physician.[8]

Ryno continued the Smith medical dynasty through his four sons, all of whom became physicians: Berwick Bruce Smith (1826–60), M.D. University of Maryland, 1849; Nathan Ryno Smith, Jr. (1831–56), M.D. University of Maryland, 1855; Alan Penniman Smith (1840–98), M.D. University of Maryland, 1861; and Walter Prescott Smith (1842–63), M. D. University of Maryland, 1863.

Berwick Bruce Smith, a pathologist, died of infections received in the dissecting room. Nathan Ryno Smith Jr. died only one year after graduating from the University of Maryland where his father taught. Alan Penniman Smith was a professor of surgery at Maryland and a member of the Johns Hopkins University board of trustees where he knew Osler and helped with the establishment of the medical school there. Alan was the only son to outlive Ryno Smith. Although the Smith family roots ran deep in New England, Baltimore during the Civil War was a town divided, and most of the citizenry leaned toward the Southern cause. Walter Prescott Smith, the last of Ryno's four sons, joined the Confederate forces as a surgeon immediately upon his graduation from Maryland in 1863. He died of infections received in a Confederate field hospital in Virginia.

Another grandson of the original Nathan Smith—Nathan Smith Lincoln (1828–1898), M.D. University of Maryland, 1852—became one of the most distinguished physicians in Washington, DC. During the Civil War he was surgeon-in-chief of the army hospitals in Washington. Later he was physician-in-chief at the Providence Hospital, founded by Elizabeth Ann Seton, the first American-born saint.

When Charles Guiteau shot President James A. Garfield in Washington in 1881, Dr. Lincoln was one of the first doctors on the scene. Ten doctors rushed to the Baltimore and Potomac railroad station. Dr. Willard Bliss was summoned by Secretary of War Robert Todd Lincoln whose father Abraham Lincoln had been assassinated in 1865. Bliss coveted the position of being in charge of the case, and when it became apparent that no less than twenty-two doctors were in attendance offering their services, he decided to trim the team to just a few. Bliss selected himself as physician-in-charge, Surgeon General of the Army Joseph K. Barnes, army surgeon Joseph Janvier Woodward (who had performed the autopsy on President Lincoln in 1865), and Robert Reyburn. All the other doctors, including Nathan Smith Lincoln, were dismissed.[9]

The story of Garfield's treatment and death is a sad chapter in American medical history. President Garfield suffered excruciating pain from the day of the shooting on 2 July 1881 until his death on 19 September. Charles Guiteau argued unsuccessfully at his trial that he had, in fact, shot Garfield, but it was his doctors who had killed him. Their daily probing with unsanitary instruments and fingers kept the wound from healing and insured that an infection would occur. At one point Osler's old friend D. H. Agnew from the University of Pennsylvania was called in, but lacking X-rays or other means of discovery, he could offer no help in locating and extracting the bullet. The autopsy revealed that the bullet was not lodged in Garfield's liver as the medical team thought, but was ten inches away, harmlessly surrounded by tissue in Garfield's side, a diagnosis correctly offered by Dr. Lincoln in his initial examination.[10]

Later thankful that they had been removed from the incompetent medical team, Dr. Lincoln and three other physicians published an article condemning Garfield's treatment, and Lincoln's reputation remained intact.[11] Lincoln was held in such high esteem that he became the physician to President Chester A. Arthur's family when Arthur succeeded Garfield. Nathan Smith would have been proud of his grandson.

Because he was available and willing to assist with an amputation, Nathan Smith went from behind the plow in Vermont to Harvard, Edinburgh, Glasgow, London, Dartmouth, and Yale. He advanced medical education by the founding of four medical colleges, a feat unequalled in American medical history. He became the patriarch of a family of physicians that extends to the present day. Among the many admirers who validated Smith's contributions was Sir William Osler.

NOTES

[1] *Ancestral Records and Portraits* (Baltimore: Genealogical Publishing Company, 1969), 618.
[2] Oliver S. Hayward and Constance Putnam, *Improve, Perfect, and Perpetuate: Dr. Nathan Smith and Early American Medical Education* (Hanover, NH: University Press of New England, 1998), 45.
[3] Hayward and Putnam, 272.
[4] William Osler, *Aequanimitas* (Philadelphia: P. Blakiston's Son & Co., Inc., 1932), 225.
[5] Harvey Cushing, *The Life of Sir William Osler* (Oxford: The Clarendon Press, 1925), 1: 436.
[6] Osler, 308.
[7] Osler, 449–50.
[8] Osler, 215.
[9] Charles A. Roos, "Physicians to the Presidents, and Their Patients: A Biobibliography," *Bulletin of the Medical Library Association* 49 (1961): 331.
[10] Roos, 330.
[11] Smith Townshend, C.B. Purvis, N. S. Lincoln, and P.S. Wales, "President Garfield's Wound and Its Treatment," *Walsh's Retrospect* 2 (1881): 623–633.

CHAPTER NINE

Osler and Whitelaw Reid

WILLIAM OSLER AND WHITELAW REID (1837–1912), the American ambassador to the Court of St. James's, had several interesting connections. They arrived in England the same year, 1905. They both received honorary degrees from Oxford and Cambridge. They both married women from distinguished families. They both were close friends with Mark Twain. They both led lives of accomplishment in their professions. In England Osler and Reid became friends, and Osler served as Reid's physician.[1]

Whitelaw Reid was the son of a farmer in Ohio. He graduated with scientific honors from Miami University of Ohio in 1856 at age 18. As a journalist based in Washington, DC, he covered political topics for the *Cincinnati Times,* the *Cleveland Herald,* and the *Cincinnati Gazette.* He became a fervent Republican and backed Abraham Lincoln for the presidency in 1860.

When the Civil War began, he joined the Union forces and was commissioned a captain. He served on the staff of General George McClellan as aide-de-camp, but his primary contribution to the war was his detailed reporting back to the Ohio papers of conditions in the field, especially during the battles of Shiloh and Gettysburg.

Immediately following the Civil War, he toured the South for one year and published *After the War* in 1866, in which he asserted that white Southerners had not changed their views and that re-unification of the country would remain difficult. He thought the South continued to harbor its resentment of the late President Lincoln and his Republican Party. Indeed, he accurately forecast the post-war hegemony of the Democratic Party in the American South that would last more than a century.

Because Reid was well-connected politically and had proven his worth as a newspaperman, the legendary editor of the *New York Tribune,* Horace Greeley (1811–1872), hired him in 1868 as an assistant editor, and Reid's career as a public man began to accelerate. He moved rapidly from being an assistant editor, to chief editorial writer, to managing editor.

He ran the *New York Tribune* when Horace Greeley campaigned unsuccessfully for the presidential nomination for the Liberal Republican Party in 1872.[2]

Greeley's health deteriorated and he died shortly after his electoral defeat, so Reid borrowed money from industrialist Jay Gould to buy controlling shares in the *Tribune* and became editor-in-chief. This was a common practice in those days for the editor to own controlling shares so that his personal fortune was directly tied to the success of the newspaper.

Reid was determined to keep the *Tribune* an independent organ and to report political corruption wherever it occurred, including the Republican Party. He insisted so many times that the *Tribune* was not a Republican organ that he was lampooned frequently in other publications by the famous cartoonist Thomas Nast who usually depicted Reid with some sort of musical instrument such as a violin or drum with a sign on it saying, "This is not an organ."

To his credit, Reid's editorials did not sink to sensationalism at a time of yellow journalism, and his writing did much to redefine the role of editors and newspapers in shaping public opinion. Despite his attempts to remain neutral, in his position as editor and publisher of one of the nation's leading newspapers, he accrued great political influence. By the way, in 1886 the forward-looking Reid was the first to use the linotype composing machine invented by Ottmar Mergenthaler to print the *Tribune*. This new printing process allowed the *Tribune* to reach a mass market quicker than any other newspaper at that time.[3]

In 1881 he married Elizabeth Mills, daughter of Darius Ogden Mills, one of the wealthiest men in American. He had made his fortune during the California Gold Rush of 1849 and founded the California Bank in San Francisco. With his marriage to Elizabeth Mills, Reid never had to worry about money again. In England, Osler frequently asked Mrs. Reid for donations to causes he deemed worthy.

In 1889, Reid accepted the post of minister to France where his skill at negotiations persuaded the French government to enter into some treaties with the United States that seem quite contemporary. For example, he extracted an agreement from the French government to end its prohibition against the importing of American meat, and he obtained new extradition treaties for criminals who might otherwise go unpunished.

In 1892, Republicans selected Reid as Benjamin Harrison's vice-presidential running mate, but his ticket lost to Democrat Grover Cleveland. When Republican William McKinley won the White House back in the next election in 1896, Reid was once again restored to positions of influence. McKinley wanted Reid as his Secretary of State, but a Republican Senator from New York, Thomas Platt, who felt that he had not been treated well in the pages of the *Tribune*, effectively blocked Reid's confirmation in the Senate.

Following the Spanish–American War in 1898, McKinley appointed Reid to lead the American delegation for the peace negotiations with Spain. And in 1905, President Theodore Roosevelt named Reid as the United States ambassador to Great Britain, and it was here that Osler and Reid became close.

When Reid arrived as ambassador, Osler wasted no time in asking his help in obtaining contributions from Americans for Oxford's Bodleian Library. In November 1905, Osler wrote to Reid, "Many thanks for your letter of the 14th. The Bodleian is used so extensively by Americans and they are so well treated and so warmly welcomed, that this would be an appropriate occasion for some of them to express their appreciation in a practical manner. . . ."[4]

Cambridge University had conferred a degree on Reid in 1902 when he served as the special ambassador to King Edward VII's coronation, and in 1907 Lord Curzon of Oxford invited him to receive the Doctor of Civil Laws degree on 26 June along with other degree recipients including Mark Twain, Rudyard Kipling, and French sculptor Auguste Rodin.

Chapter 3 contains a discussion of Mark Twain's visit to Oxford and his luncheon with the Oslers at 13 Norham Gardens, but prior to that event Reid and Mark Twain spent time together in London just a few days before the Incaenia at Oxford.

Reid's friendship with Twain went as far back as 1869 when Reid wrote an editorial blasting the city fathers of Memphis, Tennessee, for having reneged on funds to repay a group of Northern investors for paving the streets of downtown Memphis.[5] Mark Twain's father-in-law Jervis Langdon had personally invested $500,000 in the venture. Following Reid's editorial, the city honored its debt, and Twain and Reid were close correspondents from that time on and frequently found themselves at banquets and other events.

On 21 June 1907, Whitelaw Reid hosted a dinner for Mark Twain at Dorchester House, the ambassador's residence in London. Among the guests were Alfred, Lord Tennyson's son Hallam; Sir Arthur Conan Doyle of Sherlock Holmes fame; Bram Stoker, the author of *Dracula*; and Alfred Austin, the Poet Laureate of England. Imagine the conversation and wit around that table.

That Whitelaw Reid was one of the most successful U.S. ambassadors to Great Britain cannot be denied. When a change of administration occurs, the new president normally appoints his own ambassadors, especially to the coveted position in London. In anticipation of such a change, Secretary of State Elihu Root wrote to Reid in May 1909 as Theodore Roosevelt was about to turn over the presidency to William Howard Taft,

> I have appreciated very highly the admirable tact and good judgment and wisdom with which you have managed the many delicate and important matters which have arisen and have had to be disposed of in whole or in part in London while you have been Ambassador. . . . Taken all in all I am sure that you ought to look back over your period of service in the distinguished list of American Ambassadors to Great Britain with the greatest satisfaction.[6]

But President Taft did not desire a change, and when word reached England that Reid would remain, His Majesty King Edward VII sent a letter to Reid on 10 December 1909, saying,

> I rejoice to learn that your tenure of office as Ambassador of the United States to the Court of St. James's is likely to continue. There is no one who

could fill such a post with greater distinction than yourself, and I personally rejoice that one who I have learned to know as a friend will not now leave my country.

   Believe me,
     Very sincerely yours,
      EDWARD R.[7]

Meanwhile the friendship of Osler and Reid flourished. In October 1909, Osler gave a lecture at the London School of Tropical Medicine. Presiding was Whitelaw Reid, who introduced Osler as a "very excellent example of what the [United] States could do with a Canadian when caught young."[8]

A month later Reid hosted a luncheon at Dorchester House in honor of Henry Watterson, editor of *The Louisville Courier-Journal*. Although most of the guests were editors of London's principal newspapers and government officials, Reid wanted his friend Osler to attend, and he did.[9]

In October 1912, a month that included two transatlantic crossings and a speech in Wales, Reid was exhausted. He called upon his friend Osler. They had known each other for seven years, and Osler had become Reid's physician. Reid had a history of bronchial trouble, and it returned accompanied by asthma. The sickness was complicated by painful neuralgia. Reid's staff implored Osler to come from Oxford during this crisis to attend to him. This insistence is reminiscent of Walt Whitman's disciples fanning out across Philadelphia in search of Osler in 1888 when it appeared that Whitman was near death. Reid's biographer says, "Sir William Osler stimulated him with the assurance that absolute rest and careful life in the open air would effect a cure. [Osler reminded him] also that he had passed his seventy-fifth birthday."[10]

Reid wrote to an American friend (Mrs. Cowles), "Osler tells me that all my recent trouble is due entirely to overwork and especially to my hurried trip to America, to do my duty as a member of the board of Regents [of New York], and to my hurried trip back, to Wales, to tell a small portion of the truth about Thomas Jefferson at the University College."[11]

Two months later, his last illness began on 3 December 1912 with the end coming on 15 December. On the day of Reid's death, Osler said,

> I have had a worrying week. First with a succession of Examiners from outside who have to be looked after, but more particularly with Whitelaw Reid's illness. I had to go to town every evening as I seemed to be of greater comfort to him than his London doctors. He passed away peacefully this morning. He had a long & useful innings & will be much missed here.[12]

His Majesty King George V, who had succeeded Edward VII, wrote to President Taft, "It is with the deepest sorrow that I have to inform you of the death of Mr. Whitelaw Reid, at noon today. As your Ambassador in this country his loss will be sincerely deplored, while personally I shall mourn for an old friend of many years' standing for whom I had the greatest regard and respect. The Queen and I sympathize most warmly with Mrs. Whitelaw Reid in her heavy sorrow."[13]

Normally such condolences would be conveyed by the Foreign Office, so the king's letter breaks with precedent and is an indication of his high regard for Reid. Further, the king insisted that a memorial service be held in Westminster Abbey with all of the foreign diplomatic corps in attendance. This was another break with precedence because the traditional site for such memorials would have been St. Paul's. The king requested and received permission to convey Reid's body home to America on a British navy vessel. From London a special train took Reid's body to Portsmouth where, as a final tribute, all the ships in the harbor flew the United States ensign as the warship left port.[14]

Thus ended a lifetime of achievement: Civil War officer; innovative newspaper editor; chief ambassador to the peace conference that ended the Spanish–American War; nominee for Vice President of the United States; ambassador to both France and Great Britain; and—at the last—friend and patient of Sir William Osler.

NOTES

[1] Ironically, before he went to England Osler was the attending physician to the British ambassador to the United States, Lord Pauncefote. See "Pauncefote Very Ill." *The Los Angeles Times*, May 16, 1902, 1.
[2] William Harlan Hale, *Horace Greeley: Voice of the People* (New York: Harper & Brothers, 1950), 303.
[3] Samuel Eliot Morison and Henry Steele Commager, *The Growth of the American Republic* (New York: Oxford University Press, 1962), 2:193–4.
[4] Harvey Cushing, *The Life of Sir William Osler* (Oxford: The Clarendon Press, 1925), 2:30.
[5] Victor Fischer and Michael B. Frank, eds., *Mark Twain's Letters* (Berkeley: University of California Press, 1992), 3:264–5.
[6] Royal Cortissoz, *The Life of Whitelaw Reid* (New York: Charles Scribner's Sons, 1921), 2:393.
[7] Cortissoz, 2:394.
[8] Cushing, 2:192.
[9] "Reid Gives Luncheon for Watterson," *New York Times*, November 2, 1909, 4.
[10] Cortissoz, 2:449.
[11] Cortissoz, 2:449.
[12] Cushing, 2:342.
[13] Cortissoz, 2:450.
[14] Cortissoz, 2: 453–4.

CHAPTER TEN

Osler and John Keats

AMONG OSLER'S FAVORITE POETS was John Keats, one of the canonical British Romantic Poets, and one who also had extensive medical training in the early nineteenth century. His brief, tragic life and his ill-fated love are legendary. Not so well known is the fact that Keats received extensive medical training as an apothecary-surgeon. The knowledge of his impending death at an early age, combined with his knowledge of medicine, enabled him to produce masterful poems, three of which illustrate his creative power.

Keats is permanently enshrined in the pantheon of British Romantic Poets along with Wordsworth, Shelley, Lord Byron, Coleridge, and William Blake. Osler acknowledged that Keats was one of his favorite poets in his talk "John Keats: The Apothecary Poet," delivered to the Johns Hopkins Historical Club in October 1895. Osler describes Keats as "one of the clearest, sweetest, and strongest singers of the century, whose advent sets at naught all laws of heredity."[1] Osler refers to heredity because Keats's father kept the stables at the sign of the "Swan and Hoop" in Moorgate Pavement, having married the daughter of the innkeeper. His father died when Keats was eight years old, but his mother's family had money, so the future poet was provided for and well-educated.[2]

In 1810, when Keats was fifteen, his mother died of consumption as tuberculosis was then called. His guardian placed him as an apprentice to Thomas Hammond, an apothecary–surgeon, and he remained with Hammond for almost five years.

The tri-partite divisions of the medical profession into physicians, surgeons, and apothecaries often blurred in those days. Physicians were university trained and earned the degree of M.D.; surgeons received intensive training in the hospitals and were addressed as "Mr."; apothecaries, in the lower tier, could qualify after an apprenticeship with a master, but they could also become apothecary–surgeons with additional training.

In July 1815, Parliament passed the Apothecary Act requiring all aspiring apothecaries to serve one year at a hospital. This new law sought to improve the level of training of apothecaries which had come increasingly under attack by the Royal College of Physicians and the Royal College of Surgeons. And so, in October 1815 Keats entered the Guy's Hospital for a year's study consisting of one course each in anatomy and physiology, two courses in the theory and practice of medicine, two courses in chemistry, and one in materia medica.[3] The senior lecturer in anatomy, Astley Cooper, was one of the masters of English surgery with a reputation as a superb surgeon and a master teacher.[4] Cooper noticed Keats's demonstrated proficiency for surgery and awarded him a coveted "dressership," a singular honor among the medical students because that meant that he could directly assist with surgeries.[5] Walt Whitman was a "wound dresser" during the American Civil War, but all he did was change bandages and clean wounds; Keats as a dresser actually performed several surgeries unassisted and unsupervised. He acquired the technical skills for surgery, but he could not deal emotionally with the suffering of the patients, particularly children, as they came under the scalpel without the benefit of anesthesia.[6]

WAS KEATS A DOCTOR?

At the end of his year of training, he passed the four examinations required and became a Licentiate of the Society of Apothecaries.[7] His credentials as a Licensed Apothecary–Surgeon were significant for that time. The Society of Apothecaries was incorporated as a City Livery Company by royal charter from James I on 6 December 1617 in recognition of apothecaries' skills in compounding and dispensing medicines. The Society of Apothecaries is the oldest guild in existence in the City of London. They acquired their Apothecaries Hall in Black Friars Lane in 1632. Although Keats was a legally ratified member of the medical profession, he was not a doctor in the sense of an MD. Trying to sort out just exactly what Keats's medical status would have been in his day almost two-hundred years ago is complicated, but the closest equivalent would be what we call today a general practitioner. He could have seen patients at his "surgery," the doctor's office, he could have prescribed and dispensed medicine, and he could have performed surgery, limited as it was in those days.

In 1917, during World War I, the Society of Apothecaries had the responsibility of certifying Apothecaries' Assistants or Dispensers, the majority of whom were women assisting in the war effort. At the completion of their studies, they were qualified to dispense medicine for a pharmacist. One of those who sat for and passed the examination was a young woman who drafted her first detective novel that year, and so it was that her knowledge of drugs, especially poisons, would later serve Agatha Christie well in her literary career.[8]

KEATS AND FANNY BRAWNE

In 1818, Keats met Fanny Brawne (1800–1865). Their relationship is one of the great love stories of the literary world. She was a beautiful, vivacious girl of eighteen, full of laughter and dancing. Keats was smitten the moment he met her, and she became devoted to Keats. But, she came from a substantial London family—a cousin was the legendary Beau Brummell[9]— and Keats had no money. His inheritance was tied up endlessly in the courts, so he never enjoyed financial independence. Any money that came to him he gave to his younger brother George who had emigrated to Louisville, Kentucky, in 1818 where he died of consumption.

That same year, 1818, Keats's brother Tom died from the family disease, tuberculosis, which had taken their mother. On the night of 3 February 1820, Keats himself coughed up blood. Using his trained medical eye, he said, "I know the colour of that blood. It's arterial blood. There's no mistaking that colour. That blood is my death warrant. I must die."[10] A series of hemorrhages weakened him in the spring and summer of 1820, and his condition declined so much that a group of friends took up a subscription to send him to Italy where consumptives often went to escape the English winters and sit in the Mediterranean sun and bake their ravaged lungs.

They engaged the services of Joseph Severn an artist whom Keats had first met in 1815 to accompany him to Italy. His parting from Fanny Brawne was unspeakably sad; they both knew that they would never see each other again. The idea that Keats could defeat the tuberculosis was folly and they knew it. He died in Rome on 23 February 1821 and was buried in the Protestant Cemetery. He asked that Severn arrange for an inscription on his tombstone to read, "Here lies one whose name was writ in water."

Fanny Brawne, an unmarried widow, grieved for Keats

for six years. She dressed in widow's weeds and sequestered herself from the London social scene. Twelve years after Keats's death, she finally did marry at age 33 a Portugese aristocrat twelve years her junior (the age Keats was when he died) and lived in Europe most of her life. She wore Keats's engagement ring for the rest of her life and said not a word to her husband of her love for Keats for seven or eight years after their marriage. When her husband noticed a portrait of Keats at a friend's home and inquired about him, Fanny equivocated and said that he had been an acquaintance many years before. That was as much as she ever said to her husband about Keats.[11]

POETRY AND MEDICAL IMAGERY

Some of his better-known poems contain medical or pharmacopoeial imagery. Keats does not employ his knowledge of drugs in a showy or ostentatious way. His imagery complements the themes of the various poems.

In "Ode on Melancholy," the speaker urges the reader not to reject melancholy, not to try to escape pain. Melancholy, like pleasure, is a heightened sensibility, and to the Romantic poets, feeling is all. The first stanza reads

> No, no! go not to Lethe, neither twist
>   Wolf's-bane, tight rooted, for its poisonous wine;
> Nor suffer thy pale forehead to be kist
>   By nightshade, ruby grape of Proserpine;
> Make not your rosary of yew-berries,
>   Nor let the beetle, nor the death-moth be
>   Your mournful Psyche, nor the downy owl
> A partner in your sorrow's mysteries;
>   For shade to shade will come too drowsily,
>   And drown the wakeful anguish of the soul.

Wolf's-bane and nightshade are poisonous plants that Keats would have studied in his botany classes. Yew-berries are symbols of death. In line six he mentions the beetle, likely a reference to the black beetle or scarab that the Egyptians often placed in tombs as symbols of resurrection. The death-moth refers to the death's-head moth which has markings on its back that resemble a skull. All these negative images associated with Melancholy seem bleak, but the speaker insists that Pleasure cannot exist without Melancholy; they are inseparable, and if we would enjoy Pleasure, we must glut our sorrow whenever Melancholy appears.

In "Ode to a Nightingale," Keats uses the nightingale as a symbol of Immortality. Clearly autobiographical, this poem also uses medical imagery. In the opening lines the speaker says,

> My heart aches, and a drowsy numbness pains
> > My sense, as though of hemlock I had drunk,
> Or emptied some dull opiate to the drains
> > One minute past, and Lethe-wards had sunk.

Hemlock, of course, is a poisonous herb, most famously used by Socrates in ancient Athens. The speaker wishes for the "drowsy numbness" that "some dull opiate" might bring to alleviate his suffering, something to make him sink "Lethe-wards." Lethe is a river in Hades whose waters cause forgetfulness. Our words lethargy and lethargic originate from Lethe.

In stanza two, the speaker fancies that he will turn to wine, "a draught of vintage," to help him fade away in the night with the nightingale.

In stanza three he deplores

> The weariness, the fever and the fret
> > Here, where men sit and hear each other groan;

> Where palsy shakes a few, sad, last gray hairs,
>   Where youth grows pale, and spectre-thin, and dies.

In stanza four he rejects poisons, opiates, and wine and turns to Poetry. In stanza six Keats doubtless speaks of his own weakened, tubercular condition when the speaker calls upon Death to "take into the air my quiet breath." This poem contrasts the pain and suffering of being mortal with the ease and comfort of Immortality.

A final example of Keats's use of somatic imagery occurs in his famous "Ode on a Grecian Urn." Here the urn becomes the symbol for Immortality, just as the nightingale was in the previous poem. The speaker envies the bride and bridegroom depicted on an ancient urn. In stanza two he says that the wedding couple can never consummate their love. They are inches away from kissing, but not quite:

> Bold Lover, never, never cast thou kiss,
>   Though winning near the goal—yet do not grieve;
> She cannot fade, though thou hast not thy bliss,
>   For ever wilt thou love, and she be fair!

In stanza three the speaker describes what it is like to be mortal. Unlike these lovers frozen on the urn, we mortals must suffer

> All breathing human passion far above,
>   That leaves a heart high-sorrowful and cloy'd,
>   A burning forehead, and a parching tongue.

The poem asks, would you rather be like the wedding couple, frozen through all time, forever young and beautiful, but never kissing, or would you rather be mortal, consummate your love, and suffer all the "burning forehead, and a parching tongue"? The speaker concludes that mortality with all its attendant troubles is superior to immortality.

Keats's literary reputation rests on a half-dozen great odes, lyrical poems of enormous power, and a few longer poems such as "The Eve of St. Agnes," "Lamia," and "La Belle Dame Sans Merci." Inevitably two questions arise: What might his poetic output have been had he not died young? And, conversely, did the knowledge of his rapidly approaching mortality spur him on to produce in 1819 poem after poem at a frenetic pace. By the time he became unable to write poetry at age twenty-four, his writings exceeded the accomplishments of Chaucer, Shakespeare, and Milton when they were that age. Keats is a magnificent poet who, in abandoning his medical training, secured his place among the British poets.

NOTES

[1] William Osler, *An Alabama Student; And Other Biographical Essays* (New York: Oxford University Press, 1909), 37.
[2] Dorothy Hewlett, *A Life of John Keats*, 2nd ed. rev. (New York: Barnes & Noble, Inc., 1950), 15.
[3] Hewlett, 37.
[4] Hillas Smith, *Keats and Medicine* (Isle of Wight, England: Cross Publishing, 1995), 54.
[5] Aileen Ward, *John Keats: The Making of a Poet* (New York: The Viking Press, 1963), 50–51.
[6] Ward, 102.
[7] Hewlett, 43.
[8] Janet P. Morgan, *Agatha Christie: A Biography* (New York: Alfred A. Knopf, 1985), 71.
[9] Joanna Richardson, *Fanny Brawne: A Biography* (London: Thames and Hudson, 1952), 3.
[10] Ward, 347.
[11] Richardson, 126–27.

Ode on Melancholy (1819)

1

No, no, go not to Lethe, neither twist
  Wolf's-bane, tight-rooted, for its poisonous wine;
Nor suffer thy pale forehead to be kiss'd
  By nightshade, ruby grape of Proserpine;
Make not your rosary of yew-berries,
  Nor let the beetle, nor the death-moth be
    Your mournful Psyche, nor the downy owl
A partner in your sorrow's mysteries;
    For shade to shade will come too drowsily,
      And drown the wakeful anguish of the soul.

2

But when the melancholy fit shall fall
  Sudden from heaven like a weeping cloud,
That fosters the droop-headed flowers all,
  And hides the green hill in an April shroud;
Then glut thy sorrow on a morning rose,
  Or on the rainbow of the salt sand-wave,
    Or on the wealth of gloved peonies;
Or if they mistress some rich anger shows,
    Emprison her soft hand, and let her rave,
      And feed deep, deep upon her peerless eyes.

3

She dwells with Beauty—Beauty that must die;
  And Joy, whose hand is ever at his lips
Bidding adieu; and aching Pleasure nigh,
  Turning to poison while the be-mouth sips:
Ay, in the very temple of Delight
  Veil'd Melancholy has her Sovran shrine,
    Though seen of none save him whose strenuous tongue
  Can burst Joy's grape against his palate fine;
His soul shall taste the sadness of her might,
    And be among her cloudy trophies hung.

Ode to a Nightingale (1819)

1

My heart aches, and a drowsy numbness pains
  My sense, as though of hemlock I had drunk,
Or empties some dull opiate to the drains
  One minute past, and Lethe-wards had sunk:
'Tis not through envy of they happy lot,
  But being too happy in thine happiness,—
    That thou, light-winged Dryad of the trees,
      In some melodious plot
  Of beechen green, and shadows numberless,
    Singest of summer in full-throated ease.

2

O, for a draught of vintage! That hath been
  Cool'd a long age in the deep-delved earth,
Tasting of Flora and the country green,
  Dance, and Provençal song, and sunburnt mirth!
O for a beaker full of the warm South,
  Full of the true, the blushful Hippocrene,
    With beaded bubbles winking at the brim,
      And purple-stained mouth;
  That I might drink, and leave the world unseen,
    And with thee fade away into the forest dim:

3

Fade far away, dissolve, and quite forget
  What thou among the leaves hast never known,
The weariness, the fever, and the fret
  Here, where men sit and hear each other groan;
Where palsy shakes a few, sad, last gray hairs,
  Where youth grows pale, and spectre-thin, and dies;
    Where but to think is to be full of sorrow
      And leaden-eyed despairs,
  Where Beauty cannot keep her lustrous eyes,
    Or new Love pine at them beyond tomorrow.

4

Away! Away! For I will fly to thee,
   Not charioted by Bacchus and his pards,
But on the viewless winges of Poesy,
   Though the dull brain perplexes and retards:
Already with theee! Tender is the night,
   And haply the Queen-Moon is on her throne,
      Cluster'd around by all her starry Fays;
         But here there is no light,
Save what from heaven is with the breezes blown
   Through verdurous glooms and winding mossy ways.

5

I cannot see what flowers are at my feet,
   Nor what soft incense hangs upon the boughs,
But, in embalmed darkness, guess each sweet
   Wherewith the seasonable month endows
The grass, the thicket, and the fruit-tree wild;
   White hawthorn, and the pastoral eglantine;
      Fast fading violets cover'd up in leaves;
         And mid-May's eldest child,
The coming musk-rose, full of dewy wine,
   The murmurous haunt of flies on summer eves.

6

Darkling I listen; and for many a time
   I have been half in love with easeful Death,
Call'd him soft names in many a mused rhyme,
   To take into the air my quiet breath;
Now more than ever seems it rich to die,
   To cease upon the midnight with no pain,
      While thou art pouring forth thy soul abroad
         In such an ecstasy!
   Still wouldst thou sing, and I have ears in vain—
      To thy high requiem become a sod.

7
Thou was not born for death, immortal Bird!
  No hungry generations tread thee down;
The voice I hear this passing night was heard
  In ancient days by emperor and clown:
Perhaps the self-same song that found a path
  Through the sad heart of Ruth, then, sick for home,
    She stood in tears amid the alien corn;
      The same that oft-times hath
  Charm'd magic casements, opening on the foam
    Of perilous seas, in faery lands forlorn.

8
Forlorn! The very word is like a bell
  To toll me back from thee to my sole self!
Adieu! The fancy cannot cheat so well
  As she is fam'd to do, deceiving elf.
Adieu! Adieu! Thy plaintive anthem fades
  Past the near meadows, over the still stream,
    Up the hill-side; and now 'tis buried deep
      In the next valley glades:
  Was it a vision, or a waking dream?
    Fled is that music:—Do I wake or sleep?

Ode on a Grecian Urn (1819)

Thou still unravished bride of quietness!
  Thou foster-child of silence and slow time,
Sylvan historian, who canst thus express
    A flow'ry tale more sweetly than our rhyme:
What leaf-fringed legend haunts about thy shape
    Of deities or mortals, or of both,
      In Tempe or the dales of Arcady?
    What men or gods are these? What maidens loth?
What mad pursuit? What struggle to escape?
    What pipes and timbrels? What wild ecstasy?

Heard melodies are sweet, but those unheard
    Are sweeter; therefore, ye soft pipes, play on;
Not to the sensual ear, but, more endeared,
    Pipe to the spirit ditties of no tone:
Fair youth, beneath the trees, thou canst not leave
    Thy song, nor ever can those trees be bare;
      Bold Lover, never, never canst thou kiss,
Though winning near the goal -yet, do not grieve;
      She cannot fade, though thou hast not thy bliss,
    For ever wilt thou love, and she be fair!

Ah, happy, happy boughs! that cannot shed
    Your leaves, nor ever bid the Spring adieu;
And, happy melodist, unwearied,
    For ever piping songs for ever new;
More happy love! more happy, happy love!
    For ever warm and still to be enjoyed,
      For ever panting and for ever young;
All breathing human passion far above,
      That leaves a heart high-sorrowful and cloyed,
    A burning forehead, and a parching tongue.

Who are these coming to the sacrifice?
  To what green altar, O mysterious priest,
Lead'st thou that heifer lowing at the skies,
  And all her silken flanks with garlands drest?
What little town by river or sea-shore,
  Or mountain-built with peaceful citadel,
    Is emptied of its folk, this pious morn?
And, little town, thy streets for evermore
  Will silent be; and not a soul to tell
    Why thou art desolate, can e'er return.

O Attic shape! Fair attitude! with brede
  Of marble men and maidens overwrought,
With forest branches and the trodden weed;
  Thou, silent form, dost tease us out of thought
As doth eternity: Cold pastoral!
  When old age shall this generation waste,
    Thou shalt remain, in midst of other woe
  Than ours, a friend to man, to whom thou sayst,
"Beauty is truth, truth beauty, -that is all
  Ye know on earth, and all ye need to know."

CHAPTER ELEVEN

Osler and John Donne

AMONG OSLER'S DIVERSE READING, the works of John Donne (1571–1631) occupy a special place. Donne stands between Shakespeare and Milton chronologically and enjoys with them status in the pantheon of English poets. William Osler and John Donne shared several interests and, in many ways, had similar backgrounds with regard to religious disquiet, love of literature, and an interest in one's approach to death as the ultimate life experience.

Donne had the misfortune of being born into a Catholic family at a time of most intense anti-Catholic sentiments in England. When he was in his twenties, Donne converted to the Church of England, partly out of piety but also partly out of a desire to get ahead, perhaps a court appointment or as a writer among a discerning reading public. In becoming a convert to the Church of England, Donne did not become anti-Catholic, although he frequently expressed anti-Jesuit thoughts. Osler never switched his allegiance from the English Church, but he did experience some attenuation of his observation of the rituals of the organized church, choosing to conduct his hospital rounds on Sunday morning to avoid having to endure the liturgical aspects of a church service. Osler's alteration of his intention to become an Anglican priest represents not so much an apostasy as a professional course correction. In his much-admired address "A Way of Life" delivered at Yale in April 1913, he adjures the students, "Begin the day with Christ and His prayer—you need no other. Creedless, with it you have religion; creed-stuffed, it will leaven any theological dough in which you stick."[1]

Donne was a brilliant preacher at a time when the public admired oratory. His sermons consistently linked mankind with God. King James I—yes, the King James who commissioned the English translation of the Bible—often heard Donne's sermons and took an interest in his ecclesiastical career that culminated in Donne's becoming the Dean of St. Paul's. As a poet, Donne shows a remarkable ability to bring together the sacred and secular portions of his life, just as Osler, it seems to me, had a remarkable ability to connect experiences however disparate they might seem. In Donne's day poets wrote about elevated themes and experiences, but Donne could infuse his poetry with the trivial and the mundane,[2] often venturing into the medical realm with somatic imagery of sickness, vomit, excrement, and the like, found unexpectedly in a sonnet about religious devotion. Similary, Osler could leave behind the day's dreadful sights he must have seen in the pathology lab and the autopsy room and deliver an eloquent address full of literary allusion that same evening. They understood that making both connections and detachments were a necessary dichotomy.

An example of a poem that reflects Donne's thinking on death is *Holy Sonnet 10* (1633) in which the speaker personifies Death and "kills" him by arguing that death is a welcome relief and rest from labor. Death is not to be feared but welcomed:

> Death, be not proud, though some have callèd thee
> Mighty and dreadful, for thou art not so;
> For those whom thou think'st thou dost overthrow

> Die not, poor Death, nor yet canst thou kill me.
> From rest and sleep, which but thy pictures be,
> Much pleasure; then from thee much more must flow,
> And soonest our best men with thee do go,
> Rest of their bones, and soul's delivery.
> Thou art slave to fate, chance, kings, and desperate men,
> And dost with poison, war, and sickness dwell,
> And poppy or charms can make us sleep as well
> And better than thy stroke; why swell'st thou then?
> One short sleep past, we wake eternally
> And death shall be no more; Death, thou shalt die.

Another interesting link of Osler with Donne is that Donne's contemporary biographer was Izaak Walton (1593–1683).[3] Walton was the author of *The Compleat Angler* (1653), and every Oslerian knows that one of Osler's affectionate nicknames for his son Revere was "Isaac" because of his love for fishing. In a letter written in 1905, Osler brags that Revere "is a crazy fisherman & thinks of nothing but his rod & reels and lines. He has caught about eight of the fish Izaak Walton describes."[4]

Like Osler, Donne married a woman from a distinguished family, but his secret marriage to Ann More in 1601, when he was twenty-nine and she seventeen, so scandalized London society that his father-in-law had him briefly imprisoned. She bore him twelve children, and for many years he lived in poverty, barely able to feed his children. He had a large family, no money, and no prospects.

BIATHANATOS

In 1608, during this period of despair he wrote a defense of suicide entitled *Biathanatos,* although it would not be published until 1646, fifteen years after his death. The spelling of the title is important. Greek *bios* means life, but *bia* means force or violence. Thanatos is the Greek word for death; thus, *Biathantos* does not mean life-death but dying by violence, or, specifically, suicide. The word suicide, by the way, did not come directly from the Latin, as is commonly supposed; it is a fairly recent word, unknown in Donne's time.[5]

The full title is *Biathanatos. A Declaration of that Paradoxe, or Thesis, That Self-homicide is not so naturally Sin, that it may never be otherwise.* He cites historical and Biblical precedents illustrating the desirability of committing self-homicide, as suicide was then called. This is the earliest expression of Donne's death wish, but he did not publish it because it was simply too inflammatory and heretical with its endorsement of self-destruction.[6]

Donne was not advocating suicide as a solution to one's problems, but he was seeking to remove suicide as a sin as it was then perceived by all established Western religions, particularly the Roman and English Churches, as well as under English law. Donne wanted to afford salvation to those who felt that they had no alternative other than self-homicide. His own age was full of turmoil: labor riots, general filth and unsanitary conditions in the cities, sexually transmitted diseases brought to the port of London from all over the world. Suicides among young men Donne's age were common.[7]

Regarding Osler's much-discussed, controversial satire "The Fixed Period," in which Osler endorses the wisdom of chloroforming people when they reach the age of sixty, most scholarly attention focuses on Osler's use of Anthony Trollope's novel *The Fixed Period,* but before mentioning Trollope, Osler says, "In his *Biathanatos* Donne tells us that by the laws of certain wise states sexagenarii were precipitated from a bridge, and in Rome men of that age were not admitted to the suffrage and they were called *Depontani* because the way to the senate was *per pontem,* and they from age were not permitted to come thither."[8] The writings of John Donne were at least as important as Trollope's novel in assisting Osler with the writing of "The Fixed Period."

Osler was delighted to add a 1646 first edition of *Biathanatos* to his library, and that copy is today in the Osler Library.[9] One way to try to understand Osler's active mind is to look at the miscellany of items that Osler habitually inserted into copies of his beloved books. There one can find such items as newspapers articles, jottings, marginalia, and personal letters—often from famous or later-to-be-famous figures from his time. In his copy of *Biathanatos,* Osler inserted several items. He made particular note of this passage from near the end of Donne's treatise:

> And thus retaining ever in our minds, that our example is Christ, and that he dyed not constrained, it shall suffice to have learned by these places, that in Charitie men may dye so, and have done, and ought to doe. (194)

To think of Christ's death as the world's most famous suicide is not only shocking to the sensibilities of some, but an unacceptable blasphemy to others. And yet, Christ's only purpose in coming to earth was to die; his entire life was a prelude to the impact that his death would create. Osler turns to his King James Bible and juxtaposes with Donne's thought this quotation from the book of Romans (Ch. 5.7): "For scarcely for a righteous man will one die; yet peradventure for a good man some would even dare to die." Think of the early Christians dying in the Colosseum.

Osler's note in *Biathanatos* acknowledges that the term

Biathanati was "a term applied derisively to the early Christians, many of whom courted martyrdom." Given our recent experience with "suicide bombers" in the troubled Middle East, we can understand that the particular form of suicide that leads to martyrdom could be—in a certain cultural and geographical context— a desirable end to life.

COUNT NOGI OF JAPAN

In 1912, Osler seems to have entered a period near the end of his life when he was interested in what he called "sacrificial suicide." He clipped from the London *Times* and inserted into his copy of *Biathanatos* two cuttings on the suicide of Count Nogi of Japan that occurred that year. Once again we see Osler's capacity for wide-ranging reading and intellectual inquiry.

Count Maresuke Nogi (1843–1912) was a Japanese general whose heart never left the nineteenth century and whose spirit, even while he was alive, dwelt with the ancient samurai warriors of the *bushido* tradition. Osler certainly knew of Count Nogi because the old general had visited England in 1910 where he twice reviewed parades of the Boy Scouts under the direction of Lord Robert Baden-Powell. Baden-Powell praised Nogi's sense of self-sacrifice as a soldier.

In the war between Japan and Russia in 1904, Nogi commanded the Japanese troops that captured Port Arthur (jutting westward from the Chinese mainland into the Yellow Sea near Korea Bay and Pohai Strait). Count Nogi's two sons were killed in the horrific assault on the Russians. Nogi served Emperor Meiji, a forward-looking samurai who modernized the army and navy, established the new capital in Tokyo, and became Japan's first constitutional monarch. Nogi became a tutor and mentor to Meiji's grandson, later to become Emperor Hirohito. When Emperor Meiji died in 1912, Nogi and his wife committed ceremonial suicide together as an act of loyalty to their leader. Dressed in formal Japanese garb, the couple stood facing portraits of the late Emperor Meiji and the present Emperor Yoshihito and their two sons killed at Port Arthur. Countess Nogi, under her husband's supervision, committed hara-kiri, disembowelment. He followed by slitting his throat. Count Nogi willed his body to medical science.

Osler read with interest—enough interest to clip the articles and save them—the public reaction to Nogi's suicide. The London *Times* correspondent in Tokyo wrote that "Public opinion unanimously concedes that Count Nogi's suicide was inspired by the loftiest motives, but there is a marked tendency to regard the act as typifying a practice no longer in consonance with the spirit of the times." The reporter quotes the Japanese newspaper *Asahi* as saying, "We cannot restrain our admiration of Count Nogi, but we cannot extol the act as an example for the people. Let this be the last act of the kind which adorns the history of Bushido."

The second item relating to the suicide of Count Nogi is an editorial in the *Times*, "Morals in East and West." It begins, "The suicide of Count Nogi seems, no doubt, an act entirely natural and right to the Japanese. In England attempted suicide is a crime usually punished lightly or not at all; but still a crime for which a man may be placed in the dock." Later the editorial offers the opinion that, "The Christian gave a supreme example of spiritual freedom when he sacrificed his life to his faith; and devotion to any cause in the face of material danger and physical pain is admired all the world over as a proof of spiritual freedom." The writer draws a distinction between the Eastern and Western cultures in maintaining personal spiritual freedom:

They prove that freedom by maintaining their manners, even when in great grief or pain. But they prove it most of all by dying when they can no longer remain triumphant over circumstances, or when circumstances disgust them. We are apt to assume that suicide is a cowardly way out of a difficulty; but the Chinese and Japanese recognize no duty to live, and they suspect cowardice rather in what seems to them an unseemly persistence in living.

CARDINAL GIBBONS

Also inserted in Osler's copy of *Biathanatos* is an article by James Cardinal Gibbons (1834–1921), published in 1907 in *The Century Illustrated Monthly Magazine*.[10] Osler knew and liked Gibbons; they were next-door neighbors in Baltimore. Gibbons's article offers just the sort of intellectual content that Osler loved: many classical and Biblical allusions. He rails against "the instinctive horror and disgrace attached to deeds of self-destruction" (401). He condemns people facing painful and debilitating deaths who commit suicide by requesting from their doctors a pharmaceutical release from life. He also takes aim at the physicians who advocate euthanasia, saying, "There is no doubt that some degenerate members of that noble and humane profession would be willing to pronounce sentence of death, and I fear that a clergyman would also be on hand, who would be as tolerant and accommodating" (406).

Osler and Cardinal Gibbons had an interesting relationship. They shared an alley and frequently encountered each other coming or going. On one occasion the press created a fictitious feud between science and religion using Osler and Gibbons as representatives of the two camps. *The Washington Post* published on April 20, 1913, an article with an enticing title: "Dr. Osler Shocks Prelate." Osler delivered the dedicatory address at the Pipps Pychiatric Clinic at the Johns Hopkins Hospital on April 19, 1913. He was quoted as saying, "Ninety-nine percent of our fellow creatures, when in trouble, sorrow, or sickness, trust to charms, incantations, and to the saints. Many a shrine has more followers than Pasteur; many a saint more believers than Lister. Mentally the race is still in leading strings."[11]

According to the article, Cardinal Gibbons's response to Osler's equating the saints with charms and incantations was to announce that he was shocked: "Scientists sometimes make statements such as that of Dr. Osler. . . . These scientific specialists think their statements should go unchallenged, but this one of Dr. Osler shall not, and I shall write to him asking him to retract it." The Cardinal pointed out that Pasteur was a devout Catholic.

Osler replied, "I am no enemy of the saints. I will talk to my friend, the cardinal, about this as soon as I get back." Osler was on his way to Yale University to deliver the Silliman Lecture, "A Way of Life." Osler's first biographer, Harvey Cushing, said this entire exchange was nonsense, calling the article "a fictitious interview," an invented controversy that sought to capitalize on the notoriety resulting from Osler's "The Fixed Period" speech in 1905.[12] Osler and Gibbons recognized that the press had hoped to create friction where none existed, and the two remained good friends.

Osler had become so aligned by the popular media with the idea of the attractiveness of an early, voluntary or involuntary death, that he became a target for reporters looking for any opportunity for a good story. In December 1905, following "The Fixed Period Speech" and its subsequent publicity, Osler found himself again represented as indifferent to the anxiety of those approaching death. An article in the *Chicago Daily Tribune* of December 20, 1905, entitled "Deathbed Visions a Hoax?" has as its sub-head "Dr. Osler Scouts Theory of Mortal Glimpses of Beyond." The article's lead sentence reads, "Dr. William Osler, the man who wants the aged hustled graveward, is out with a really important and interesting declaration. In his latest book he says: '"Deathbed" visions, believed in by thousands and of which there are scores of supposed authentic records, are plain nonsense.'"[13] Osler is quoted here from his collection of essays *Counsels and Ideals* published in England and America in 1905. The article serves no purpose other than to provoke further controversy capitalizing on "The Fixed Period" episode.

Years later, in 1918, during World War I, Osler and Gibbons were still on good terms, so much so that Osler felt that he could publish a letter in the London *Times* calling on the Cardinal to use his influence with the large Irish Catholic populations in the United States and Canada to persuade the young men of Ireland to answer the call to arms.[14] The Irish strongly opposed conscription into the British forces. He also wrote a draft of an open letter—never sent and found among Osler's papers after his death—to Cardinal Gibbons. The letter begins warmly: "Dear Cardinal, Claiming the privilege of an old friend, & for many years your next-door neighbour, may I address you an open letter on a subject that I know you have at heart—an Irish settlement." He compliments Gibbons: "No man in the United States wields the same personal influence as your Eminence."

CONCLUSION

Certainly attempts to classify Osler as in favor of a premature death were exaggerations, but what were Osler's thoughts concerning suicide? We began by looking at some items that Osler cared enough about to clip and insert into his copy of Donne's *Biathanatos*, an argument justifying suicide in special circumstances. Osler augmented Donne's treatise with articles praising the loyalty and sense of personal honor that prompted the suicide of Count Nogi, balanced with an article by his friend Cardinal Gibbons allowing no justification for suicide under any circumstances and directing particular indignation towards physicians who might accede to the request of terminally ill patients who seek to commit suicide with their doctor's assistance. Fortunately, Osler also inserted some comments that reveal his own views on this inflammatory subject:

> All reasonable people must deplore the increase of suicide in our modern civilization, so often a selfish and cowardly act; but the fact of Count Nogi gives pause to the wholesale condemnation and raises the question under what circumstances, if any, a man in his right senses may rightly disregard the canon against self-slaughter. Animated by a spirit not easy for the Western mind to enter, Count Nogi did it as an act of sacrifice; and so, too, it may be to the Western man. It has been my lot to see the end of scores of the rashly importunate, weary of breath, and to see but few that roused any feelings other than pity for the folly (or the *folie!*), or anger at an undutiful mutiny. But among those few there were some that I could not condemn, others that I could not but admire, and even, maybe, approve.
>
> It is not surprising in the Lucretian age when to many death is the "be all and the end all," that we find men who, when beaten to the pit (*Jul. Caes.*, v, 5, 23), deem it more worthy to leap in than tarry to be pushed.[15]

Remember that this is a private note, not a public speech,

and therefore it carries the weight of credibility. These are Osler's thoughts about suicide, prompted by Donne's *Biathanatos* and other readings. He does not condemn those who commit suicide. He says he admires some and approves of others. Osler closely monitored his own final illness, assessing his condition daily. And seeing that he was progressing inevitably towards the end and that it was not far away, he did not commit suicide. Given the indications contained in his private thoughts, had Osler not been comfortably surrounded by loving friends and relatives, his books and letters, had he not known that a swift end was near, he might have seriously entertained the idea of suicide.

NOTES

[1] William Osler, "A Way of Life," in *Osler's "A Way of Life" and Other Addresses, with Commentary and Annotations,* Sigeaki Hinohara and Hisaw Niki, eds. (Durham, NC: Duke University Press, 2001), 16.
[2] Joan Bennett, *Five Metaphysical Poets* (Cambridge: Cambridge University Press, 1964), 15–16.
[3] Izaak Walton, *The Life and Death of Dr. Donne, Late Deane of St. Pauls London,* Introduction to *LXXX Sermons* (London: Richard Royston and Richard Marriott, 1640).
[4] Harvey Cushing, *The Life of Sir William Osler* (Oxford: Clarendon Press, 1925), 2: 14.
[5] David Daube, "The Linguistics of Suicide," *Philosophy and Public Affairs* 1 (1972), 419.
[6] Donald Ramsey Roberts, "The Death Wish of John Donne," *PMLA* 62 (1947), 969.
[7] Clara Lander, "A Dangerous Sickness Which Turned to a Spotted Fever, " *Studies in English Literature, 1500–1900* 11 (1971), 105.
[8] William Osler, "The Fixed Period," in *Aequanimitas* (Philadelphia: P. Blakiston's Son, 1932), 382.
[9] *Biathanatos* is item number 4742 in the *Bibliotheca Osleriana* (Kingston and Montreal: McGill-Queens University Press, 1969), 428.
[10] James Cardinal Gibbons, "The Moral Aspects of Suicide," *The Century Illustrated Monthly Magazine* 73 (1907), 401–407.
[11] "Dr. Osler Shocks Prelate," *The Washington Post* April 20, 1913, 11.
[12] Cushing, 2: 353.
[13] "Deathbed Visions a Hoax?" *Chicago Daily Tribune, December 20, 1905:* 1.
[14] J.B. Lyons, "Osler and Ireland," *Osler Library Newsletter* June 1993, 2.
[15] William Osler, "John Donne," in *Bibliotheca Osleriana* (Kingston and Montreal: McGill-Queens University Press, 1969), 428.

WORKS CITED

Adelson, Betty M. *The Lives of Dwarfs: Their Journey from Public Curiosity toward Social Liberation.* New Brunswick, NJ: Rutgers University Press, 2005.

Altick, Richard D. *The Scholar Adventurers.* New York: The Macmillan Company, 1950.

Ancestral Records and Portraits. Baltimore: Genealogical Publishing Company, 1969.

Beck, Ian. " 'The Body's Purpose': Browning, and So to Beddoes." *Browning Society Notes* 14, no. 1 (1984): 2–20.

Bennett, Joan. *Five Metaphysical Poets.* Cambridge: Cambridge University Press, 1964.

Bliss, Michael. *William Osler: A Life in Medicine.* New York: Oxford University Press, 1999.

Braverman, Rachel. "Philadelphia's Unknown Master." *History Today* (October 1993): 2–3.

Bryan, Charles S. *Osler: Inspirations from a Great Physician.* New York: Oxford University Press, 1997.

Bucke, Richard Maurice. *Cosmic Consciousness: A Study in the Evolution of the Human Mind.* 1901. New York: Citadel Press, 1993.

Carlin, David. "Sir Thomas Browne's *Religio Medici* and the Publishing House of Ticknor & Fields." *Osler Library Newsletter* (October 1998): 3–4.

Carson, John. "Mark Twain's Georgia Angel-Fish Revisited." *Mark Twain Journal* 36, no. 1 (1998): 16–18.

Clinton, Catherine. *The Other Civil War: American Women in the Nineteenth Century.* New York: Hill and Wang, 1984.

Cogan, Frances B. *All-American Girl: The Ideal of Real Womanhood in Mid-Nineteenth Century America.* Athens: University of Georgia Press, 1989.

Collard, Edgar Andrew. *Montreal Yesterdays.* Toronto: Longman's, 1962.

Cooley, John, ed. *Mark Twain's Aquarium: The Samuel Clemens Angelfish Correspondence, 1905–1910*. Athens: The University of Georgia Press, 1991.

Coxe, Louis. *Enabling Acts: Selected Essays in Criticism*. Columbia, MO: The University of Missouri Press, 1976.

Crenner, Christopher. *Private Practice: In the Early Twentieth-Century Medical Office of Dr. Richard Cabot*. Baltimore: The Johns Hopkins University Press, 2005.

Cushing, Harvey. *The Life of Sir William Osler*. New York: The Clarendon Press, 1925.

Daube, David. "The Linguistics of Suicide." *Philosophy and Public Affairs* 1 (1972), 387–437.

"Deathbed Visions a Hoax?" *Chicago Daily Tribune*, December 20, 1905: 1.

Defies, Esther Phoebe. *A Browning Primer*. Port Washington, NY: Kennikat Press, 1970.

Donner, H.W., "Introduction," *Plays and Poems of Thomas Lovell Beddoes*. London: Routledge and Kegan Paul Ltd., 1950.

Donovan, Josephine. *Sarah Orne Jewett*. New York: Frederick Ungar Publishing Co., Inc., 1980.

Dowden, Edward. *Robert Browning*. Port Washington, NY: Kennikat Press, 1970.

Dwight, Eleanor. *Edith Wharton: An Extraordinary Life*. New York: Harry N. Abrams, Inc., 1994.

Earnest, Ernest. *The American Eve in Fact and Fiction, 1775–1914*. Urbana: University of Illinois Press, 1974.

Fischer, Victor, and Michael B. Frank, eds. *Mark Twain's Letters*. Berkeley: University of California Press, 1992.

Frankenberger, Charles. "The Collection of Portraits Belonging to the College." *The Jeffersonian* 27 (1915): 1–10.

Fried, Michael. *Realism, Writing, Disfiguration: On Thomas Eakins and Stephen Crane*. Chicago: The University of Chicago Press, 1987.

Garnett, Richard. "Beddoes, Thomas." *The Dictionary of National Biography*. London: Humphrey Milford, 1921–22.

Gibbons, James Cardinal. "The Moral Aspects of Suicide." *The Century Illustrated Monthly Magazine* 73 (1907), 401–407.

Golden, Richard L. *The Works of Egerton Yorrick Davis, MD; Sir William Osler's Alter Ego*. Montreal: Osler Library, 1999.

Golden, Richard L. *A History of William Osler's "The Principles and Practice of Medicine."* Montreal: Osler Library, 2004.
Gosse, Edmund, ed. *The Complete Works of Thomas Lovell Beddoes.* London: The Fanfrolico Press, 1928.
Hale, William Harlan. *Horace Greeley: Voice of the People.* New York: Harper & Brothers, 1950.
Hacker, Carlotta. "Emily Howard Stowe," in *The Canadian Encyclopedia,* vol. 3. Edmonton, Alberta: Hurtig Publishers, 1985.
Hayward, Oliver S., and Constance Putnam. *Improve, Perfect, and Perpetuate: Dr. Nathan Smith and Early American Medical Education.* Hanover, NH: University Press of New England, 1998.
Herman, Chad. "Daughters, Wives, and Mothers: Women's Oppression in Thomas Lovell Beddoes' *The Brides' Tragedy.*" *Mount Olive Review* 6 (1992): 115–121.
Hewlett, Dorothy. *A Life of John Keats,* 2nd ed. rev. New York: Barnes & Noble, Inc., 1950.
Irvine, William, and Park Honan. *The Book, the Ring, and the Poet: A Biography of Robert Browning.* New York: McGraw-Hill Book Company, 1974.
Jack, Ian. *English Literature, 1815–1832.* Oxford: The Clarendon Press, 1963.
Jackel, Susan. "Women's Suffrage," in *The Canadian Encyclopedia,* vol. 3. Edmonton, Alberta: Hurtig Publishers, 1985.
Jewett, Sarah Orne. *A Country Doctor.* New York: Bantam, 1999.
Johns, Elizabeth. *Thomas Eakins: the Heroism of Modern Life.* Princeton: Princeton University Press, 1983.
Lander, Clara. "A Dangerous Sickness Which Turned to a Spotted Fever." *Studies in English Literature, 1500–1900* 11 (1971), 89–108.
Lanier, Doris. "Mark Twain's Georgia Angel-Fish." *Mark Twain Journal* 24, no. 1 (1986): 4–16.
Leon, Philip W. *Walt Whitman and Sir William Osler: A Poet and His Physician.* Toronto: ECW Press, 1995.
Lundin, John. "T.L. Beddoes at Göttengen." *Studia Neophilologica* 43 (1971): 484–499.
Lyons, J.B.. "Osler and Ireland." *Osler Library Newsletter* (June 1993): 1–3.

"Mark Twain Explains." *The New York Times,* December 25, 1881: 3.
Morgan, Janet P. *Agatha Christie: A Biography.* New York: Alfred A. Knopf, 1985.
Moylin, Christopher. "T. L. Beddoes, Romantic Medicine, and the Advent of Therapeutic Theater." *Studia Neophilologica* 63 (1991): 181–188.
Nation, Earl F., Charles G. Roland, and John P. McGovern, eds. *An Annotated Checklist of Osleriana.* Kent, OH: Kent State University Press, 1976.
"Osler Shocks Prelate." *The Washington Post,* April 20, 1913: 11.
Osler, William. *Aequanimitas; with Other Addresses.* Philadelphia: P. Blakiston's Son & Co., 1932.
Osler, William. *An Alabama Student; and Other Biographical Essays.* New York: Oxford University Press, 1909.
Osler, William. "John Donne" in *Bibliotheca Osleriana.* Kingston and Montreal: McGill-Queen's University Press, 1969.
Osler, William. *Osler's "A Way of Life" and Other Addresses, with Commentary and Annotations,* Shigeaki Hinohara and Hisae Niki, eds. Durham, NC: Duke University Press, 2001.
Osler, William. *The Principles and Practice of Medicine.* New York: D. Appleton and Company, 1892.
Porter, Fairfield. *Thomas Eakins.* New York: George Braziller, Inc., 1959.
Rechnitzer, Peter. *R.M. Bucke: Journey to Cosmic Consciousness.* Markham, Ontario: Fitzhenry & Whiteside, 1994.
"Reid Gives Luncheon for Watterson." *New York Times,* November 2, 1909, 4.
Richardson, Joanna. *Fanny Brawne: A Biography.* London: Thames and Hudson, 1952.
Roberts, Donald Ramsay. "The Death Wish of John Donne." *PMLA* 62 (1947), 958–976.
Roos, Charles A. "Physicians to the Presidents, and Their Patients: A Biobibliography." *Bulletin of the Medical Library Association* 49 (1961): 291–360.
Sakula, Alex. *The Portraiture of Sir William Osler.* London: The Royal Society of Medicine, 1991.
Salsbury, Edith, ed. *Suzy and Mark Twain Family Dialogues.* New York: Amereon House, 1965.

Salveson, Paul. *Loving Comrades: Lancashire's Links to Walt Whitman*. Bolton, England: Worker's Educational Association, 1984.

Schiller, F.C.S. *Humanism: Philosophical Essays*. London and New York: Macmillan, 1903.

Sewell, Darrel. "Self Portrait," in *Thomas Eakins (1844-1916) and the Heart of American Life*, ed. John Wilmerding. London: The National Portrait Gallery, 1994.

Silverman, Mark E., T. Jock Murray, and Charles S. Bryan, eds. *The Quotable Osler*. Philadelphia: American College of Physicians, 2003.

Smith, Hillas. *Keats and Medicine*. Isle of Wight, England: Cross Publishing, 1995.

Stephens, James, Edwin L. Beck, and Royall H. Snow, eds. *Victorian and Later English Poets*. New York: American Book Company, 1949.

Strachey, Lytton. *Books and Characters: French and English*. New York: Harcourt, Brace and Company, 1922.

Symons, Arthur. *An Introduction to the Study of Browning*, 2nd ed. rev. Port Washington, NY: Kennikat Press, 1970.

Townshend, Smith, et al. "President Garfield's Wound and Its Treatment." *Walsh's Retrospect* 2 (1881): 623-633.

Traubel, Horace. *With Walt Whitman in Camden*, vol. 2. New York: Rowman and Littlefield, 1961.

Twain, Mark. "Marjorie Fleming, the Wonder Child." *Harper's Bazaar*, December 1909, reprinted in Paul Fatout, ed., *Mark Twain Speaks for Himself*. West Lafayette, IN: Purdue University Press, 1978.

Wagner, Frederick B. Jr. *The Twilight Years of Lady Osler: Letters of a Doctor's Wife*. Canton, MA: Science History Publications, 1985.

Wallis, Faith, and Blake Gopnik. "Finding Osler's Letters in the Osler Library: A Preliminary Report and Some Discoveries." *Osler Library Newsletter* (February 1988): 1-3.

Walton, Izaak. "The Life and death of Dr. Donne, Late Deane of St. Pauls London." Introduction to *LXXX Sermons*. London: Richard Royston and Richard Marriott, 1640.

Ward, Aileen. *John Keats: The Making of a Poet*. New York: The Viking Press, 1963.

INDEX

Aben-Ezra, Abraham-ben-Meir, 93–95. *See also* Browning, Robert
Agnew, D. H., 115
Alcott, Louisa May, 64
American Psychiatric Association, 1
Anthony, Susan B., 63

Baden-Powell, Robert 152
Beddoes, Thomas, 43
Beddoes, Thomas P., 52, 53
Beddoes, Thomas Lovell, 43–55 passim; *The Brides' Tragedy,* 44; *Death's Jest-Book,* 44, 45; in Baden, 45; in Basel, 45; in Berlin, 45; in Frankfort, 45; in Göttingen, 45; in Zurich, 45; and suicide, 45-46; and curari, 50, 54
Biathanatos (Donne), 149–152, 158
Blackwell, Elizabeth, 62
Bliss, Willard, 117
Bolton College, 7–14
Bowdoin College, 113
Brawne, Fanny, and John Keats, 134–135
British Classical Association, 12

Brown, John, 29, 30–32; "Marjorie Fleming," 30–32; "Rab and His Friends," 30–31
Browne, Thomas, 60; *Religio Medici,* 60
Browning, Elizabeth Barrett, 55, 93–94
Browning, Robert, 59, 79; and Osler 93–101 passim; "Rabbi Ben Ezra," 93–101
Bucke, Richard M., 1; *Cosmic Consciousness,* 3–4, 55

Carson, John, 35
Christie, Agatha, 133
Clemens, Samuel, *see* Twain, Mark
Cleveland, Grover, 123
Coleridge, Samuel Taylor, 43
Cooper, Astley, 132

Dartmouth College medical school, 112, 118
Darwin, Charles, 43, 60
Darwin, Erasmus, 43
Donne, John, 147–158 passim; *Biathanatos,* 149–152, 156–58; converts to Church of England, 147; Dean of St.

Paul's, 148; and somatic imagery, 148
Doyle, Sir Arthur Conan, 125

Eakins, Thomas, 17–26 passim; *The Gross Clinic* 17, 19-23; *The Agnew Clinic* 17, 23–25
Edinburgh, 100, 112, 118
Edward VII (king of England), 124, 125

Faraday, Michael, 43
Fields, Annie, and Sarah Orne Jewett, 59
Fields, James T., 59, 64
Forman, Harry Buxton, 55
Fullerton, Morton, 73

Galen, 79, 80
Garfield, James A., treatment of, 116–18
Garrett, Mary E., 60
George V (king of England), 127
Gibbons, James Cardinal, 154–57
Goodhue, Josiah, 111
Gosse, Edmund, 46; *The Poetical Works of Thomas Lovell Beddoes*, 46; *The Letters of Thomas Lovell Beddoes*, 46, 55
Greeley, Horace, 122
Gross, Samuel D., 19, 115
Gross, Samuel W., 22, 115

Halsted, H.A., 25
Harrison, Benjamin, 123

Harvard University medical school, 61, 62, 111, 112, 118

James I (king of England), 133, 148, 151
James, Henry ("Harry"), 74–77
James, Henry, 73–84 passim
James, William, 74
Jefferson Medical College, 18, 19, 20, 21, 115
Jewett, Sarah Orne, and Osler, 60–69 passim; *A Country Doctor*, 64–69
John Hopkins Historical Club, 131
Johns Hopkins University medical school, 6, 24, 60, 61, 69, 100, 116
Johnston, John, 8–11

Keats, John, 131–138 passim; as apothecary–surgeon, 132-133; death of, 134; and medical imagery, 135–138; "Ode on a Grecian Urn," 137–38; "Ode on Melancholy," 135–37; "Ode to a Nightingale," 136–37
Kelly, H. A., 25
Kipling, Rudyard, 32–33, 124

Lincoln, Abraham, 117
Lincoln, Nathan Smith, 116–18
Lincoln, Robert Todd, 117
London (Ontario) Asylum for the Insane, 1–3

Index

Loyola, Ignatius, 81-82

McGill University medical school, 1, 46, 97
McKinley, William, 123
Medical Society of London, 112
Mitchell, S. Weir, 24

Nast, Thomas, 122
National American Woman's Suffrage Association, 63
New Haven Medical Association, 98
Nogi, Maresuke, suicide of, 152–54; Osler's thoughts on, 157
Nunnally, Frances, 35

"Ode on a Grecian Urn" (Keats), 137–38, 144–45
"Ode on Melancholy" (Keats), 135–36, 140
"Ode to a Nightingale" (Keats), 136-37, 140–43
Osler, Grace Revere (Mrs. William), 22, 32, 33, 115
Osler Library of the History of Medicine, 74, 151
Osler, Revere (son), 33
Osler, William, "Aequanimitas," 100; "Books and Men, 115; and Bucke, 1–4; and Browning, 93–101; and Count Nogi, 152-54, 157; corresponds with Edith Wharton, 75–78; and Keats, 131–138; "John Keats: The Apothecary Poet," 132; "Doctors and Nurses," 60; "The Fixed Period," 150–51, 155–56; "Man's Redemption of Man," 100; "The Old Humanities and the New Science, 12; "On the Educational Value of the Medical Society," 98; *The Principles and Practice of Medicine*, 26, 69; "Some Aspects of American Medical Bibliography," 114; "Teaching and Thinking," 97; "Teacher and Student," 96; thoughts on suicide, 157; treats Henry James, 74–78; treats Walt Whitman, 5–7; treats Whitelaw Reid, 127–28; "A Way of Life," 99, 147–48, 155, 156; with Mark Twain at Oxford, 124

Pennsylvania Academy of Fine Arts, 18, 26

"Rabbi Ben Ezra" (Browning), 93–101
Reid, Elizabeth Mills (Mrs. Whitelaw), 123, 127
Reid, Whitelaw, 121–128 passim; as ambassador, 124; Civil War experience of, 122; and *New York Tribune*, 122–23
Ribera, 18
Roosevelt, Theodore, 124
Royal College of Physicians

(London), 132
Royal College of Surgeons (London), 132
Royal Society of Canada, 1

Sargent, John Singer, 24, 25, 26
Severn, Joseph, 134
Sixsmith, Charles F., 14
Smith, Nathan, 111–18 passim; and his legacy, 115–118; and Josiah Goodhue, 111; establishes medical school at Dartmouth, 112; establishes medical school at Yale, 112; studies abroad, 112
Smollett, Tobias, 112
Society of American Artists, 19
Society of Apothecaries (London), 133
Stoker, Bram, 125
Socrates, 96, 99
Southey, Robert, 43
Stanton, Elizabeth Cady, 63
Stowe, Harriet Beecher, 63
Strachey, G. Lytton, 47–49

Taft, William Howard, 125
Tennyson, Alfred, 55, 59, 125
Trollope, Anthony, 150-51
Twain, Mark, 29–40 passim; *Adventures of Huckleberry Finn*, 32; and his Angelfish, 34–38; and Whitelaw Reid, 121, 124, 125

University of Edinburgh, 112
University of Maryland medical school, 115
University of Minnesota medical school, 96
University of Pennsylvania medical school, 1

Velásquez, 18, 20
Vesalius, 79–81; *De Humani Corporis Fabrica*, 79, 80
"Vesalius in Zante" (Wharton), 78–84

Yale University medical school, 112–13, 118

Wallace, J. W., 11–13
Walton, Izaak, 149
Welch, W.H., 25, 61
Wharton, Edith, 73–84 passim; "Vesalius in Zante," 78–84
Wharton, Edward, 73, 74
White, J. William, 23, 24, 77
Whitman, Walt, 1–15 passim; 17, 126
Wordsworth, William, 98
Wise, Thomas J., 55

ABOUT THE AUTHOR

PHILIP W. LEON is a professor of American literature at The Citadel, Charleston, South Carolina. A graduate of Wake Forest University, he holds the Ph.D. in English from Vanderbilt University. He has published six books and has presented papers on Osler at the Royal College of Physicians (London), the Royal College of Physicians (Edinburgh), and elsewhere. He is a member of the American Osler Society, the Robert Wilson Medical History Club, and is currently president of the Waring Library Society at the Medical University of South Carolina. He has faculty status with the Department of the History and Philosophy of Medicine at the Society of Apothecaries in London.

Made in the USA
Monee, IL
06 August 2022